Invest like a Billionaire

*If you are not watching the best investor in the world,
who are you watching?*

Want to check out the best investment management companies? We pick the cream-of-the-crop portfolio managers and give you access to ALL their holdings.

CONTENTS

Warren Buffett - Berkshire Hathaway

Warren Buffett - Berkshire Hathaway

Warren Buffett

Warren Edward Buffett (born August 30, 1930, in Omaha, Nebraska) is an American investor, businessman and philanthropist. He is regarded as one of the world's greatest stock market investors, and is the largest shareholder and CEO of Berkshire Hathaway. With an estimated net worth of around US$62 billion, he was ranked by Forbes as the richest person in the world as of February 11, 2008.

Often called the "Oracle of Omaha," Buffett is noted for his adherence to the value investing philosophy and for his personal frugality despite his immense wealth. His 2006 annual salary was about $100,000, which is on the low side of senior executive remuneration in other comparable companies, and when he spent $6.7 million of Berkshire's funds on a business jet in 1989, he jokingly named it "The Indefensible" because of his past criticisms of such purchases by other CEOs. He lives in the same house in the central Dundee neighborhood of Omaha that he bought in 1958 for $31,500.

Buffett is also a noted philanthropist. In 2006, he announced a plan to give away his fortune to charity, with 83% of it going to the Bill & Melinda Gates Foundation. In 2007, he was listed among Time's 100 Most Influential People in The World. He also serves as a member of the board of trustees at Grinnell College.

Early life and Benjamin Graham

Warren Buffett was born in Omaha, Nebraska in August of 1930. As the son of a local stock broker, he was likely exposed to markets at a young age. As he got older, Buffett had a few successful entrepreneurial ventures, making him consider proceeding straight into business rather than going to college. His father, however, overruled him on this.

One of his mentors, arguably the most influential, was Benjamin Graham. Graham's philosophy had such an impact on Buffett that he enrolled in Columbia Business School to study directly under him. In Buffett's own words: "I'm 15 percent Fisher and 85 percent Benjamin Graham."

As Buffett would often say about Graham's teachings: "The basic ideas of investing are to look at stocks as business, use market fluctuations to your advantage, and seek a margin of safety. That's what Ben Graham taught us. A hundred years from now they will still be the cornerstones of investing."

Philanthropy

In June 2006, Buffett gave approximately 10 million Berkshire Hathaway Class B shares to the Bill & Melinda Gates Foundation (worth approximately USD 30.7 billion as of June 23 2006) making it the largest charitable donation in history. The foundation will receive 5% of the total donation on an annualized basis each July, beginning in 2006. Buffett will also join the board of directors of the Gates Foundation, although he does not plan to be actively involved in the foundation's investments.

He also announced plans to contribute additional Berkshire stock valued at approximately $6.7 billion to the Susan Thompson Buffett Foundation and to other foundations headed by his three children. This is a significant shift from previous statements Buffett has made, having stated that most of his fortune would pass to his Buffett Foundation. The bulk of the estate of his wife, valued at $2.6 billion, went to that foundation when she died in 2004.

His children will not inherit a significant proportion of his wealth. These actions are consistent with statements he has made in the past indicating his opposition to the transfer of great fortunes from one generation to the next. Buffett once commented, "I want to give my kids just enough so that they would feel that they could do anything, but not so much that they would feel like doing nothing".

The following quotation from 1988, respectively, highlights Warren Buffett's thoughts on his wealth and why he long planned to reallocate it:

"I don't have a problem with guilt about money. The way I see it is that my money represents an enormous number of claim checks on society. It's like I have these little pieces of paper that I can turn into consumption. If I wanted to, I could hire 10,000 people to do nothing but paint my picture every day for the rest of my life. And the GNP would go up. But the utility of the product would be zilch, and I would be keeping those 10,000 people from doing AIDS research, or teaching, or nursing. I don't do that though. I don't use very many of those claim checks. There's nothing material I want very much. And I'm going to give virtually all of those claim checks to charity when my wife and I die." (Lowe 1997:165–166)

Writings

Warren Buffett's writings include his annual reports and various articles. In his article "The Superinvestors of Graham-and-Doddsville", Buffett condemned the academic position that the market was efficient and that beating the S&P 500 was "pure chance" by highlighting a number of students of the Graham and Dodd value investing school of thought. In addition to himself, Buffett named: Walter J. Schloss, Tom Knapp, Ed Anderson (Tweedy, Brown Inc.), Bill Ruane (Sequoia Fund, Inc.), Charles Munger, Rick Guerin (Pacific Partners, Ltd.), and Stan Perlmeter (Perlmeter Investments) as having beaten the S&P 500, "year in and year out".

Berkshire Hathaway

Berkshire Hathaway (NYSE: BRK.A, NYSE: BRK.B) is a conglomerate holding company headquartered in Omaha, Nebraska, U.S., that oversees and manages a number of subsidiary companies. Berkshire Hathaway's core business is insurance, including property and casualty insurance, reinsurance and specialty nonstandard insurance. The Company averaged a 25%+ annual return to its shareholders for the last 25 years while employing large amounts of capital and minimal debt.

Warren Buffett is the company's chairman and CEO. Buffett has used the "float" provided by Berkshire Hathaway's insurance operations (a policyholder's money which it holds temporarily until claims are paid out) to finance his investments. In the early part of his career at Berkshire, he focused on long-term investments in publicly quoted stocks, but more recently he has turned to buying whole companies. Berkshire now owns a diverse range of businesses including candy production; retail, home furnishings, encyclopedias, vacuum cleaners, jewelry sales; newspaper publishing; manufacture and distribution of uniforms; and manufacture, import and distribution of footwear.

History

Berkshire Hathaway was founded as a textile manufacturing company in 1839 as the Valley Falls Company in Valley Falls, Rhode Island by Oliver Chace. Chace had previously worked for Samuel Slater, the "Founder of the American Industrial Revolution", and founded his first textile mill in 1806. In 1929 the Valley Falls Company merged with Berkshire Fine Spinning Associates, another textile company that was founded as the Berkshire Cotton Manufacturing Company in Adams, Massachusetts in 1889. The combined company was known as Berkshire Fine Spinning Associates.

In 1955 Berkshire Spinning merged with the Hathaway Manufacturing Company which was founded in 1888 in New Bedford, Massachusetts by Horatio Hathaway as a cotton milling business. Hathaway was successful in its first decades, but it suffered during a general decline in the textile industry after World War I. At this time, Hathaway was run by Seabury Stanton, whose investment efforts were rewarded with renewed profitability after the Depression. After the merger, Berkshire Hathaway had 15 plants employing over 12,000 workers with over $120 million in revenue and was headquartered in New Bedford, Massachusetts. However, seven of those locations were closed by the end of the decade, accompanied by large layoffs.

In 1962, Warren Buffett began buying stock in Berkshire Hathaway. After some clashes with the Stanton family, he bought up enough shares to change the management and soon controlled the company.

Buffett initially maintained Berkshire's core business of textile milling, but by 1967, he was expanding into the insurance industry and other investments. Berkshire first ventured into the insurance business with the purchase of National Indemnity Company. In the late 1970s, Berkshire acquired an equity stake in the Government Employees Insurance Company (GEICO), which forms the core of its insurance operations today (and is a major source of capital for Berkshire Hathaway's other investments). In 1985, the last textile operations (Hathaway's historic core) were shut down.

Berkshire facts

Berkshire's Class A shares sold for over $150,000 as of December 7, 2007, making them the highest-priced shares on the New York Stock Exchange, in part because they have never had a stock split. Shares closed over $100,000 for the first time October 23, 2006. Berkshire Class B shares trade at a fraction of the Class A prices. Despite its size, Berkshire is not included in broad stock market indexes such as the S&P 500.

Berkshire's CEO, Warren Buffett, is respected for his investment prowess and his deep understanding of a wide spectrum of businesses. His annual chairman letters are read and quoted widely. Barron's Magazine named Berkshire the most respected company in the world in 2007 based on a survey of American money managers.

As of 2005, Buffett owns 38% of Berkshire Hathaway. Berkshire's Vice-Chairman Charlie Munger also holds a stake big enough to make him a billionaire, and early investments in Berkshire by David Gottesman and Franklin Otis Booth resulted in their becoming billionaires as well. Bill Gates' Cascade Investments LLC is the second largest shareholder of Berkshire and owns more than 5% of class B shares.

Berkshire Hathaway is notable in that it has never split its shares, which not only contributed to their high per-share price but also significantly reduced the liquidity of the stock. This refusal to split the stock reflects the management's desire to attract long-term investors as opposed to short-term speculators. However, Berkshire Hathaway has created a Class B stock, with an ownership value of 1/30th of that of the original shares (now Class A) and 1/200th of the per-share voting rights. Holders of Class A stock are allowed to convert their stock to Class B, though not vice versa.

Buffett was reluctant to create the Class B shares, but did so to thwart the creation of unit trusts that would have marketed themselves as Berkshire look-alikes. As Buffett said in his 1995 shareholder letter:

"The unit trusts that have recently surfaced fly in the face of these goals. They would be sold by brokers working for big commissions, would impose other burdensome costs on their shareholders, and would be marketed en masse to unsophisticated buyers, apt to be seduced by our past record and beguiled by the publicity Berkshire and I have received in recent years. The sure outcome: a multitude of investors destined to be disappointed."

Berkshire's annual shareholders' meetings, taking place in the Qwest Center in Omaha, Nebraska, are routinely visited by 20,000 people. The 2007 meeting had an attendance of approximately 27,000. The meetings, nicknamed "Woodstock for Capitalists", are considered Omaha's largest annual event along with the baseball College World Series. Known for their humor and light-heartedness, the meetings typically start with a movie made for Berkshire shareholders. The 2004 movie featured Arnold Schwarzenegger in the role of "The Warrenator" who travels through time to stop Buffett and Munger's attempt to save the world from a "mega" corporation formed by Microsoft-Starbucks-Wal-Mart. Schwarzenegger is later shown arguing in a gym with Buffett regarding Proposition 13. The 2006 movie depicted actresses Jamie Lee Curtis and Nicollette Sheridan lusting after Munger. The meeting is also an opportunity for investors to ask Mr. Buffett questions, which is scheduled to last six hours.

The salary for the CEO is US$100,000 per year with no stock options, which is among the lowest CEO salary for other large companies in the United States.

Corporate governance

Current members of the board of directors of Berkshire Hathaway are: Howard Graham Buffett, Warren Buffett, Susan Decker, Bill Gates, David Gottesman, Charlotte Guyman, Donald Keough, Charlie Munger, Thomas S. Murphy, Ronald Olson, and Walter Scott Jr.

Company Name: Berkshire Hathaway
Shares Held, Change in Shares, and Position Change as of February 1, 2012

Ticker	Mkt Cap	Div Yield	Share Value	Shares Held	Change in Shares
AXP	$58.2B	1.5%	$6.8B	151.6M shares	No Change
BK	$24.5B	2.6%	$33.3M	1.8M shares	No Change
CDCO	$21.5M	-	$9.4M	1.5M shares	No Change
COP	$92.1B	3.8%	$1.8B	29.1M shares	*decrease of 700 shares*
COST	$35.3B	1.2%	$355.9M	4.3M shares	No Change
CVS	$55.2B	1.6%	$190.2M	5.7M shares	New Holding
DG	$14.4B	-	$169.8M	4.5M shares	**increase of 3.0M shares**
DTV	$31.7B	-	$179.6M	4.2M shares	New Holding
GCI	$3.6B	2.3%	$16.6M	1.7M shares	No Change
GD	$25.0B	2.7%	$174.3M	3.1M shares	New Holding
GE	$200.9B	3.6%	$118.4M	7.8M shares	No Change
GSK	$113.2B	4.9%	$62.4M	1.5M shares	No Change
IBM	$224.4B	1.6%	$10.0B	57.3M shares	**increase of 32.5M shares**
INTC	$136.8B	3.1%	$199.1M	9.3M shares	New Holding
IR	$10.9B	1.8%	$17.9M	636.6K shares	No Change
JNJ	$179.1B	3.5%	$2.4B	37.4M shares	*decrease of 5.2M shares*
KFT	$67.9B	3.0%	$3.0B	89.7M shares	*decrease of 9.7M shares*
KO	$153.1B	2.8%	$13.5B	200.0M shares	No Change
MA	$44.2B	0.2%	$128.4M	405.0K shares	No Change
MCO	$8.3B	1.7%	$865.2M	28.4M shares	No Change
MTB	$10.0B	3.5%	$376.2M	5.4M shares	**increase of 18.2K shares**
PG	$176.9B	3.3%	$4.9B	76.8M shares	No Change
SNY	$99.8B	3.6%	$133.3M	4.1M shares	No Change
TMK	$4.6B	1.1%	$147.7M	4.2M shares	*decrease of 0.5 shares*
UPS	$73.4B	2.7%	$90.3M	1.4M shares	No Change
USB	$53.2B	1.8%	$1.6B	69.0M shares	No Change
USG	$1.4B	-	$114.9M	17.1M shares	No Change
V	$82.0B	0.9%	$196.4M	2.3M shares	New Holding
VRSK	$6.5B	-	$73.1M	2.1M shares	No Change
WFC	$156.0B	1.6%	$8.7B	361.4M shares	**increase of 9.0M shares**
WMT	$208.6B	2.4%	$2.0B	39.0M shares	No Change
WPO	$3.0B	2.5%	$564.9M	1.7M shares	No Change
XOM	$411.4B	2.2%	$30.6M	421.8K shares	No Change

PORTFOLIO PERFORMANCE 6 MONTH

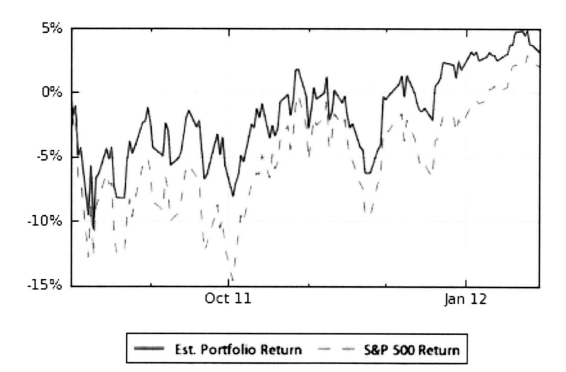

George Soros - Fund Management

George Soros - Fund Management

George Soros

George Soros (born August 12, 1930, in Budapest, Hungary, as György Schwartz) is a Hungarian-born American financial speculator, stock investor, philanthropist, and political activist.

Currently, he is the chairman of Soros Fund Management and the Open Society Institute and is also a former member of the Board of Directors of the Council on Foreign Relations. According to his own website, Soros claims his support for the Solidarity labour movement in Poland, as well as the Czechoslovak human rights organization Charter 77, contributed to ending Soviet Union political dominance in those countries. His funding and organization of Georgia's Rose Revolution was considered by Russian and Western observers to have been crucial to its success, although Soros said his role has been "greatly exaggerated." In the United States, he is known for having donated large sums of money in a failed effort to defeat President George W. Bush's bid for re-election in 2004. On BookTV, November 12, 2007, he said that he supports Barack Obama for the Democratic candidate in the 2008 election, but says that John Edwards, Hillary Clinton, or Joe Biden are all fine candidates, as well.

Soros is famously known for "breaking the Bank of England" on Black Wednesday in 1992. With an estimated current net worth of around $8.5 billion, he is ranked by Forbes as the 80th-richest person in the world.

Former Federal Reserve Chairman Paul Volcker wrote in 2003 in the foreword of Soros' book The Alchemy of Finance:

"George Soros has made his mark as an enormously successful speculator, wise enough to largely withdraw when still way ahead of the game. The bulk of his enormous winnings is now devoted to encouraging transitional and emerging nations to become 'open societies,' open not only in the sense of freedom of commerce but - more important - tolerant of new ideas and different modes of thinking and behavior."

Biography

Family

George Soros is the son of the Esperanto writer Teodoro Schwartz. Teodoro (also known as Tivadar) was a Hungarian Jew, who was a prisoner of war during and after World War I and eventually escaped from Russia to rejoin his family in Budapest.

The family changed its name in 1936 from Schwartz to Soros, in response to growing anti-semitism with the rise of Fascism. Tivadar liked the new name because it is a palindrome and because it has a meaning. Though the specific meaning is left unstated in Kaufmann's biography, in Hungarian "soros" means "next in line, or designated successor", and in Esperanto it means "will soar". His son George was taught to speak Esperanto from birth and thus is one of the rare native Esperanto speakers. George Soros later said that he "grew up in a Jewish home," and that his parents were "cautious with their religious roots." However, Soros's father was proud of his Jewish roots (which can be seen in his memoir on his experiences during the holocaust, Masquerade).

George Soros has been married and divorced twice, to Annaliese Witschak and to Susan Weber Soros. He has five children: Robert, Andrea, Jonathan (with his first wife, Annaliese), Alexander and Steven (with his second wife, Susan). His elder brother Paul Soros is an engineer, and is also a well-known philanthropist, investor, and New York socialite.

Native Hungary, and move to England

Soros was thirteen years old when Nazi Germany took military control over its wavering ally Hungary (March 19, 1944), and started exterminating Hungarian Jews in the Holocaust. Soros worked briefly for the Jewish Council, which had been established by the Nazis, to deliver messages to Jewish lawyers being called for deportation. Soros claims he was not aware of the consequence of the messages. To avoid his son being apprehended by the Nazis, his father had Soros spend the summer of 1944 living with a non-Jewish Ministry of Agriculture employee, posing as his godson.

In the following year, Soros survived the battle of Budapest, as Soviet and Nazi forces fought house-to-house through the city. Soros first traded currencies during the Hungarian hyperinflation of 1945-1946.

In 1946, Soros escaped the Soviet occupation by participating in an Esperanto youth congress in the West.

Soros emigrated to England in 1947 and graduated from the London School of Economics in 1952. While a student of the philosopher Karl Popper, Soros funded himself by taking jobs as a railway porter and a waiter at Quaglino's restaurant where he was told that with hard work he might one day become head waiter. He also worked in a mannequin factory, but was fired for being too slow at putting on the heads. He eventually secured an entry-level position with London merchant bank Singer & Friedlander.

Move to the United States

In 1956 he moved to the United States, where he worked as an arbitrage trader with F. M. Mayer from 1956 to 1959 and as an analyst with Wertheim and Company from 1959 to 1963. Throughout this time, but mostly in the 1950s, Soros developed a philosophy of "reflexivity" based on the ideas of Popper.

Reflexivity, as used by Soros, is the belief that the action of beholding the valuation of any market by its participants affects said valuation of the market in a procyclical "virtuous or vicious" circle. A current example of reflexivity in modern financial markets is that of the debt and equity of housing markets. Lenders began to make more money available to more people in the 1990s to buy houses. More people bought houses with this larger amount of money, thus increasing the prices of these houses. Lenders looked at their balance sheets which not only showed that they had made more loans, but that their equity backing the loans--the value of the houses, had gone up (because more money was chasing the same amount of housing, relatively) Thus they lent out more money because their balance sheets looked good, and prices went up more, and they lent more, etc. Prices increased rapidly, and lending standards were relaxed. The salient issue regarding reflexivity is that it explains why markets gyrate over time, and do not just stick to equilibrium--they tend to overshoot or undershoot.

Soros realized, however, that he would not make any money from the concept of reflexivity until he went into investing on his own. He began to investigate how to deal in investments. From 1963 to 1973 he worked at Arnhold and S. Bleichroeder, where he attained the position of vice-president. Soros finally concluded that he was a better investor than he was a philosopher or an executive. In 1967 he persuaded the company to set up an offshore investment fund, First Eagle, for him to run; in 1969 the company founded a second fund for Soros, the Double Eagle hedge fund.

When investment regulations restricted his ability to run the funds as he wished, he quit his position in 1973 and established a private investment company that eventually evolved into the Quantum Fund. He has stated that his intent was to earn enough money on Wall Street to support himself as an author and philosopher - he calculated that $500,000 after five years would be possible and adequate. After all those years, his net worth reached an estimated $11 billion.

He is also a former member of the Carlyle investment group.

Business

Soros is the founder of Soros Fund Management. In 1970 he co-founded the Quantum Fund with Jim Rogers. It returned 3,365% during the next ten years (42.6% per year for 10 years), and created the bulk of the Soros fortune. In 2007, the Quantum Fund returned almost 32%, netting Soros $2.9 billion.

Rogers announced his retirement from the fund in 1980.

Currency speculation

On Black Wednesday (September 16, 1992), Soros became immediately famous when he sold short more than $10 billion worth of pounds, profiting from the Bank of England's reluctance to either raise its interest rates to levels comparable to those of other European Exchange Rate Mechanism countries or to float its currency.

Finally, the Bank of England was forced to withdraw the currency out of the European Exchange Rate Mechanism and to devalue the pound sterling, and Soros earned an estimated US$ 1.1 billion in the process. He was dubbed "the man who broke the Bank of England."

The Times October 26, 1992, Monday quoted Soros as saying: "Our total position by Black Wednesday had to be worth almost $10 billion. We planned to sell more than that. In fact, when Norman Lamont said just before the devaluation that he would borrow nearly $15 billion to defend sterling, we were amused because that was about how much we wanted to sell."

According to Steven Drobny, Stanley Druckenmiller, who traded under Soros, originally saw the weakness in the pound. "Soros' contribution was pushing him to take a gigantic position," in accord with Druckenmiller's own research and instincts.

In 1997, during the Asian financial crisis, then Malaysian Prime Minister Mahathir bin Mohamad accused Soros of using the wealth under his control to punish ASEAN for welcoming Myanmar as a member. Later, he called Soros a moron. Thai nationals have called Soros "an economic war criminal" who "sucks the blood from the people".

Partners

George Soros's most successful partners at Quantum fund have been Jim Rogers, Victor Niederhoffer and Stanley Druckenmiller, all of who are famous traders in their own rights.

Insider trading charges

In 1988, he was asked to join a takeover attempt of the French bank Société Générale. He declined to participate in the bid, but did later buy a number of shares in the company. French authorities began an investigation in 1989, and in 2002 a French court ruled that it was insider trading as defined under French securities laws and fined him $2 million which was the amount that he made using the insider information.

Punitive damages were not sought because of the delay in bringing the case to trial. Soros denied any wrongdoing and said news of the takeover was public knowledge.

His insider trading conviction was upheld by the highest court in France on June 14, 2006. In December, 2006 he appealed to the European Court of Human Rights, claiming that the 14 year delay in bringing the case to trial precluded a fair hearing.

Philanthropy

Soros has been active as a philanthropist since the 1970s, when he began providing funds to help black students attend the University of Cape Town in apartheid South Africa, and began funding dissident movements behind the iron curtain.

Soros' philanthropic funding in Central and Eastern Europe mostly occurs through the Open Society Institute (OSI) and national Soros Foundations, which sometimes go under other names, e.g., the Stefan Batory Foundation in Poland. As of 2003, PBS estimated that he had given away a total of $4 billion.

He has promoted non-violent efforts to increase democracy in many countries.

The OSI says it has spent about $400 million annually in recent years.

Time Magazine in 2007 cited two specific projects - $100 million toward internet infrastructure for regional Russian universities; and $50 million for the Millennium Promise to eradicate extreme poverty in Africa - while noting that Soros has given $742 million to projects in the U.S., and given away a total of more than $6 billion.

Other notable projects have included aid to scientists and universities throughout Central and Eastern Europe, help to civilians during the siege of Sarajevo, worldwide efforts to repeal drug prohibition laws, and Transparency International. Soros also pledged an endowment of €420 million to the Central European University (CEU). The Nobel Peace Prize winner, Muhammad Yunus and his microfinance bank Grameen Bank received support from the OSI.

According to the National Review the Open Society Institute gave $20,000 in September 2002 to the Defense Committee of Lynne Stewart, the lawyer who has defended alleged terrorists in court and was sentenced to 2⅓ years in prison for "providing material support for a terrorist conspiracy" via a press conference for a client. An OSI spokeswoman said "it appeared to us at that time that there was a right-to-counsel issue worthy of our support."

In September 2006, Soros departed from his characteristic sponsorship of democracy building programs, pledging $50 million to the Jeffrey Sachs-led Millennium Promise to help eradicate extreme poverty in Africa. Noting the connection between bad governance and poverty, he remarked on the humanitarian value of the project.

He received honorary doctoral degrees from the New School for Social Research (New York), the University of Oxford in 1980, the Budapest University of Economics, and Yale University in 1991. Soros also received the Yale International Center for Finance Award from the Yale School of Management in 2000 as well as the Laurea Honoris Causa, the highest honor of the University of Bologna in 1995.

Soros Fund Management

Founded by George Soros, is a privately held corporation providing financial services and investment strategies for various funds including some controversial hedge funds such as the Quantum Group of Funds. The company's investment strategies have been based on analysis of real or perceived macroeconomic trends in various countries. Soros' companies have been accused of applying pressure on currencies to directly benefit their speculative strategies. Soros responds to these charges by saying that his funds merely take advantage of known weaknesses in the international financial system.

The hedge fund industry is quite different from the mutual fund industry. However, there is one major similarity: both industries seek to create wealth and attain high returns for clients and investors. Based on that, tracking the movements of Soros Fund Management LLC is a great strategy. For the individual investor, simply being aware of what skilled investors like George Soros and his team of managers are doing is advantageous. You may remember headlines way back in 1992 when Soros capitalized on a decline in the British pound to the tune of $1 billion. Not bad for a day's work. Although the Soros team invests differently than some of our other managers keeping an eye on any major moves they make will be interesting.

Company Name: Soros Fund Management
Shares Held, Change in Shares, and Position Change as of February 1, 2012

Ticker	Mkt Cap	Div Yield	Share Value	Shares Held	Change in Shares
AAPL	$416.9B	-	$31.8M	83.4K shares	**increase of 12.6K shares**
ACTG	$1.7B	-	$27.7M	770.1K shares	*decrease of 784.3K shares*
AGRO	$1.1B	-	$219.7M	25.5M shares	*decrease of 961.5K shares*
AMZN	$88.8B	-	$44.5M	206.0K shares	**increase of 193.3K shares**
DISH	$12.3B	-	$34.2M	1.4M shares	*decrease of 20.7K shares*
DVA	$7.5B	-	$30.6M	488.0K shares	*decrease of 16.2K shares*
EXAR	$304.6M	-	$38.1M	6.7M shares	No Change
EXTR	$300.9M	-	$21.9M	8.2M shares	*decrease of 618.6K shares*
IOC	$3.2B	-	$214.3M	4.4M shares	**increase of 425.0K shares**
MDCO	$1.0B	-	$25.3M	1.7M shares	New Holding
MRCY	$396.9M	-	$25.5M	2.2M shares	**increase of 181.4K shares**
MSI	$14.9B	1.9%	$276.4M	6.6M shares	**increase of 934.2K shares**
RL	$13.9B	0.5%	$22.6M	174.6K shares	*decrease of 820.0K shares*
VC	$2.5B	-	$70.2M	1.6M shares	**increase of 42.0K shares**
WPRT	$1.8B	-	$91.4M	3.2M shares	*decrease of 1.9M shares*

PORTFOLIO PERFORMANCE 6 MONTH

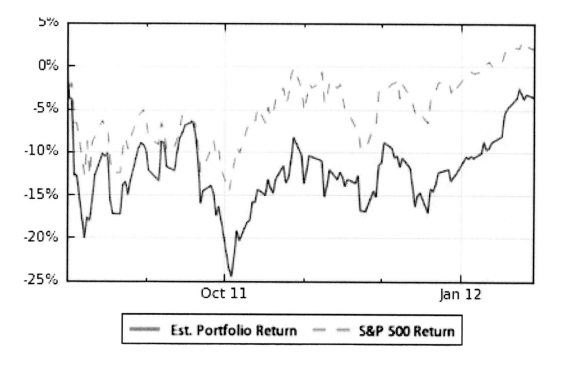

Richard Aster -
Aster Investment Management

Richard Aster - Aster Investment Management

Company Name: **Aster Investment Management**
Portfolio Manager: **Richard Aster**
Focus: **Growth Investing**

Richard Aster, manager of Meridian's growth and value funds, gained quite a name in the fund industry over the last few decades. The performance of his Meridian Growth Fund, which has been a consistent performer since its inception back in 1984 because of Aster's ability to select continually good small to mid-cap growth companies is one of the most notable accomplishments. Having run his firm for 20 years, Aster has an impressive history that shows where he learned skills necessary to become the fine money manager that he is today. Aster worked for the U.S. Treasury Department, Newburger, Loeb & Company, and the Montgomery Division at the Bank of America Securities, before starting Aster Asset Management and setting up the Meridian Growth Fund,

When picking stocks for the growth fund, Aster's strategy is not only focused on growth. Trailing earnings growth is usually at least 15%--but also on price. If a company has good growth but does not meet Aster's strict price requirements, he will not include it in this fund. This type of growth-at-a reasonable-price (GARP) strategy sends companies through the "Richard Aster Ringer," and many are not standing when they emerge--the fund traditionally holds only about 50 companies. However, you can be assured that the companies left standing are great choices.

Aster's buy-and-hold mentality, transferred over very well to the Meridian Value Fund when Aster started it ten years after the growth fund. Furthermore, this mentality makes Aster's funds prime candidates for us to follow. Aster's disinclination to flip stocks quickly, opting to allow them to develop over time and fully reach there true growth or value potential bodes well for the Investor.

Morningstar not only gave five star ratings to both the growth and value fund, but Christopher Davis, one of Morningstar's analysts, states that, the fund's steady profile has led to superb long-term results. It ranks in or near the category's top 10% for the trailing three, five, and ten years. Aster, who started the fund in 1984, has been at the helm through it all. Davis concludes by saying, that although Aster concentrates on certain sectors and has holdings of various market-cap sizes, "this fund's seasoned management, moderate volatility, and fine long-term record make it a great choice for mid- and small-growth exposure.

In addition to these factors, consistent returns, experienced management and strict stock-picking guidelines add up to Aster Capital Management being a performer to watch.

Company Name: Aster Investment Management
Shares Held, Change in Shares, and Position Change as of February 1, 2012

Ticker	Mkt Cap	Div Yield	Share Value	Shares Held	Change in Shares
ADSK	$8.2B	-	$45.7M	1.6M shares	**increase of 41.0K shares**
ARCO	$4.5B	0.8%	$51.1M	2.2M shares	*decrease of 314.3K shares*
BBBY	$15.0B	-	$57.4M	1.0M shares	*decrease of 46.5K shares*
COH	$19.9B	1.3%	$49.2M	949.7K shares	*decrease of 2.1K shares*
FDO	$6.5B	1.5%	$53.8M	1.1M shares	**increase of 323.7K shares**
MAT	$9.9B	3.1%	$79.4M	3.1M shares	*decrease of 33.8K shares*
PETM	$5.9B	1.0%	$53.3M	1.2M shares	*decrease of 1.5K shares*
ROL	$3.1B	1.5%	$49.4M	2.6M shares	*decrease of 3.2K shares*
RPM	$3.2B	3.5%	$53.0M	2.8M shares	**increase of 85.0 K shares**
SBAC	$5.0B	-	$52.3M	1.5M shares	**increase of 529.4K shares**
SLH	$3.4B	0.8%	$50.1M	991.7K shares	*decrease of 33.4K shares*
VAL	$4.0B	1.9%	$50.0M	1.6M shares	*decrease of 1.7K shares*
WCN	$3.6B	1.1%	$56.2M	1.7M shares	*decrease of 410.0K shares*
WSH	$6.7B	2.7%	$81.2M	2.4M shares	*decrease of 2.7K shares*
ZBRA	$1.9B	-	$57.0M	1.8M shares	**increase of 47.8K shares**

PORTFOLIO PERFORMANCE 6 MONTH

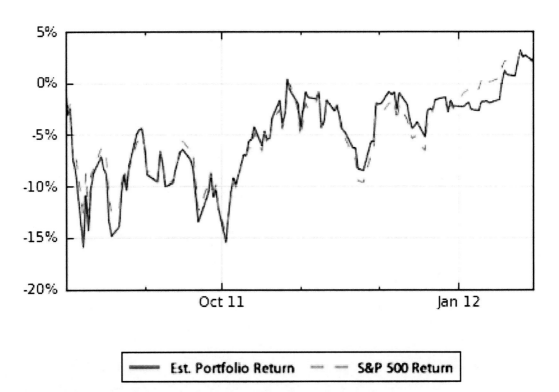

Dr. Sam Stewart - Wasatch Advisors

Dr. Sam Stewart - Wasatch Advisors

Company Name: **Wasatch Advisors Inc.**
Portfolio Manager: **Dr. Sam Stewart**
Focus: **Small and Micro Cap Growth**

This small cap-oriented fund is a true standout in the world of mutual funds. Founded in 1975 by its current CEO, Chairman and Fund Manager, Dr. Sam Stewart, Wasatch finds small companies with big growth opportunities. Stewart really defines "smart money" with his impeccable credentials. After receiving a master's in business administration and a doctorate in finance from Stanford, he has taught at the prestigious Columbia Graduate School of Business, and he holds a CFA designation. If these credentials are not convincing enough, his fund's 5- and 10-year returns have been incredible, blowing away any indices' benchmark you choose to compare against.

The Wasatch philosophy uses solid fundamental, bottom-up investing principles to find small companies with the potential to experience large gains. The premise behind focusing this is smaller companies can grow much more easily than big ones. As long as companies have solid earnings growth, both past and projected, and are trading at reasonable levels, Wasatch is willing to invest. Additionally, by periodically closing its equity funds, Wasatch is able to preserve shareholders' capital, and ensure that they will not be forced into any poor investments due to excess cash.

In addition, Wasatch's small-cap growth funds all received Lipper's maximum rating for both total and consistent returns (04/30/05). The praise from fund experts did not stop there. The Wasatch family was best summarized by Morningstar in its latest Guide to Mutual Funds (2003) by stating: "These small-cap specialists are that rare boutique that can actually manage both growth and value funds well…the firm has produced outstanding results."

Company Name:Wasatch Advisors
Shares Held, Change in Shares, and Position Change as of February 1, 2012

Ticker	Mkt Cap	Div Yield	Share Value	Shares Held	Change in Shares
CPRT	$3.0B	-	$135.0M	3.4M shares	**increase of 40.0K shares**
HIBB	$1.2B	-	$79.7M	2.4M shares	*decrease of 271.2K shares*
HITT	$1.7B	-	$65.3M	1.3M shares	**increase of 4.7K shares**
KNX	$1.4B	1.4%	$122.6M	9.2M shares	**increase of 4.2M shares**
L	$14.9B	0.7%	$64.0M	1.9M shares	**increase of 111.6K shares**
LKQX	$4.7B	-	$87.2M	3.6M shares	*decrease of 68.0K shares*
LTM	$2.0B	-	$93.5M	2.5M shares	**increase of 162.3K shares**
MNRO	$1.3B	0.8%	$63.8M	1.9M shares	*decrease of 354.7K shares*
MSCI	$3.9B	-	$79.4M	2.6M shares	**increase of 9.4K shares**
MSM	$4.7B	1.3%	$106.8M	1.9M shares	**increase of 77.2K shares**
PEET	$794.6M	-	$73.4M	1.3M shares	*decrease of 278.4K shares*
POWI	$1.0B	0.6%	$129.4M	4.2M shares	**increase of 183.1K shares**
PPO	$2.6B	-	$68.3M	1.2M shares	**increase of 212.9K shares**
ULTI	$1.7B	-	$110.6M	2.4M shares	**increase of 502.4K shares**
WMT	$208.6B	2.4%	$74.9M	1.4M shares	**increase of 141.6K shares**

PORTFOLIO PERFORMANCE 6 MONTH

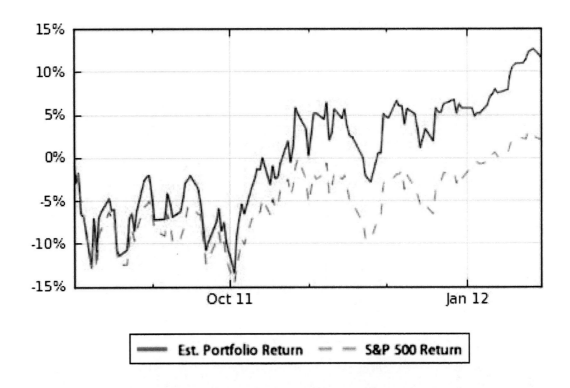

Jim W. Oberweis - Oberweis Management

Jim W. Oberweis - Oberweis Management

Company Name: **Oberweis Asset Management Inc.**
Portfolio Manager: **Jim D. Oberweis, Jim W. Oberweis**
Focus: **Small Cap Value**

Since the founding in 1986, Oberweis has become a basis in the small-cap mutual fund world. The high risk, high reward nature of this fund family is very interesting. Oberweis is run by founder Jim D. Oberweis and his son, Jim W. Oberweis. Jim W. is the day-to-day manager of the three funds this firm offers: micro-cap growth (<$250M), emerging growth (<$1B), and mid-cap growth (>$1B>$8B).

While the three different funds invest in companies of differing sizes, the overall strategy is very similar. The strategy is to invest in companies that, based on their solid business opportunities, have the potential to demonstrate incredible run ups in share price. The most important factors affecting Oberweis' investments revolve around what has become known as the "Oberweis Octagon." This is a screen that combines both qualitative and quantitative characteristics of companies. Following is a brief overview of the criteria the Oberweis Octagon requires of its potential picks.

Partially due to these eight criteria, Oberweis' flagship emerging growth fund remains in the top quintile for both five- and 15-year returns in its category. Still, there is no denying the inherently volatile nature of the "make-it-or-break-it" companies that this fund family works with. Its emerging growth fund lagged behind its peers from 1997-2000, but bounced back with vengeance, posting a 63% gain in 2003, boosting its annualized return average. The advantage this fund possesses is the shrewd stock picking ability of Jim W. Oberweis, holder of a computer science degree at the University of Illinois as well as a CFA. Because many of the companies the fund considers are high-tech companies, Jim is able to apply his knowledge of both finance, and tech industry to get a much better sense of whether the companies he analyzes are able to succeed.

Despite this fund's volatile and risky nature, we thought that keeping an eye on it was in **"INVEST LIKE A BILLIONAIRE"** Investor's best interest--as Jim W. Oberweis has remarked, it only takes a few ten   baggers (a term coined by Peter Lynch denoting a 1000% gain) to really improve a portfolio's returns.

Company Name: Oberweis Asset Management
Shares Held, Change in Shares, and Position Change as of February 1, 2012

Ticker	Mkt Cap	Div Yield	Share Value	Shares Held	Change in Shares
ACTG	$1.7B	-	$15.0M	416.4K shares	*decrease of 100.2K shares*
ARGN	$358.6M	-	$10.8M	847.9K shares	*decrease of 44.5K shares*
BODY	$426.5M	-	$5.1M	281.5K shares	**increase of 91.3K shares**
BSFT	$840.7M	-	$6.6M	216.8K shares	**increase of 45.0K shares**
FRAN	$988.7M	-	$6.7M	317.0K shares	New Holding
GIII	$468.4M	-	$5.5M	241.2K shares	*decrease of 37.7K shares*
IMAX	$1.3B	-	$6.7M	465.3K shares	**increase of 136.7K shares**
IPGP	$2.5B	-	$4.7M	109.1K shares	**increase of 23.6K shares**
MDSO	$533.7M	-	$5.2M	315.3K shares	*decrease of 20.0K shares*
MG	$629.2M	-	$6.3M	356.1K shares	**increase of 71.4K shares**
OPEN	$1.1B	-	$5.7M	123.3K shares	**increase of 45.3K shares**
SPRD	$779.1M	1.1%	$11.2M	625.4K shares	**increase of 209.4K shares**
SXCI	$3.8B	-	$7.6M	137.0K shares	*decrease of 3.9K shares*
TWIN	$360.0M	1.2%	$9.0M	336.6K shares	**increase of 85.8K shares**
WWWW	$383.5M	-	$4.9M	696.3K shares	**increase of 60.0K shares**

PORTFOLIO PERFORMANCE 6 MONTH

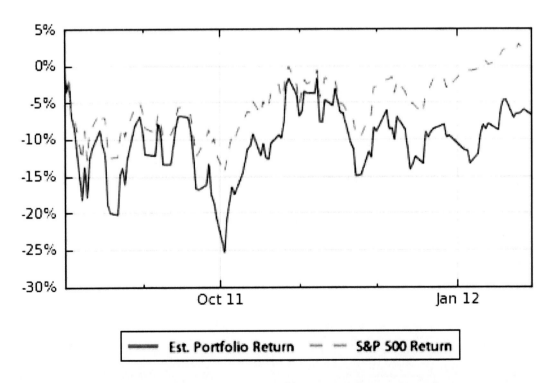

Arnie Schneider III -
Schneider Capital Management

Arnie Schneider III - Schneider Capital Management

Company Name: **Schneider Capital Management**
Portfolio Manager: **Arnie Schneider lll**
Focus: **Value Investing**

Arnie Schneider lll is the President, Chief Investment Officer and founder of Schneider Capital Management, which officially opened for business in late 1996. This management firm's investing style is a direct reflection of its founder's beliefs. The idea is that there are bargains out there which will eventually be properly priced by the market and that they simply have to be found. Schneider's deep value approach to investing is the foundation of the Schneider management philosophy.

For over twenty years, Schneider has been involved in the securities industry. What began as a career as an analyst for the Wellington Management Company, then became a senior vice-presidential position and partner. Schneider found time to earn his CFA designation as well as act as the President of the Financial Analysts of Philadelphia before starting his own money management firm. It is through his valuable experience over the years that Schneider has established steadfast values by which to invest.

Schneider believes the market's incapacity to react quickly to change means there are often undervalued stocks available. By finding a company's intrinsic value--through a stringent process of fundamental analysis including consideration of some of the basic metrics such as P/E--the astute value investor is able to profit. As you can see, Schneider's Small Cap Value fund has posted phenomenal gains over the past 3- and 5-year periods. Schneider's firm value investing principles have propelled his small-cap value fund to the top three in its class in trailing 5-year returns, an impressive feat indeed.

Even though the main small-cap fund is closed to new investors we can still take advantage of the great stock picking ability of Schneider and his money management team.

Company Name: Schneider Capital Management
Shares Held, Change in Shares, and Position Change as of February 1, 2012

Ticker	Mkt Cap	Div Yield	Share Value	Shares Held	Change in Shares
ACI	$3.0B	3.0%	$63.6M	4.4M shares	**increase of 1.2M shares**
BTU	$9.7B	1.0%	$51.3M	1.5M shares	**increase of 557.7K shares**
CLD	$1.1B	-	$30.7M	1.8M shares	**increase of 19.1K shares**
CNX	$8.2B	1.4%	$51.0M	1.5M shares	*decrease of 177.5K shares*
CSCO	$105.0B	1.2%	$42.0M	2.7M shares	*decrease of 46.1K shares*
HBAN	$4.9B	2.8%	$29.4M	6.1M shares	**increase of 1.8M shares**
JPM	$79.9B	2.7%	$27.0M	897.1K shares	*decrease of 214.5K shares*
KBH	$759.7M	2.6%	$26.5M	4.5M shares	**increase of 970.6K shares**
MGA	$9.8B	2.4%	$25.3M	768.6K shares	**increase of 294.6K shares**
NAV	$3.1B	-	$27.1M	845.0K shares	**increase of 213.5K shares**
NVR	$3.5B	-	$39.7M	65.8K shares	**increase of 1.4K shares**
PNC	$31.0B	2.4%	$28.8M	597.9K shares	*decrease of 79.3K shares*
RF	$6.6B	0.8%	$37.7M	11.3M shares	**increase of 6.2M shares**
STI	$11.0B	1.0%	$41.8M	2.3M shares	New Holding
WFC	$156.0B	1.6%	$34.9M	1.4M shares	**increase of 25.1K shares**

PORTFOLIO PERFORMANCE 6 MONTH

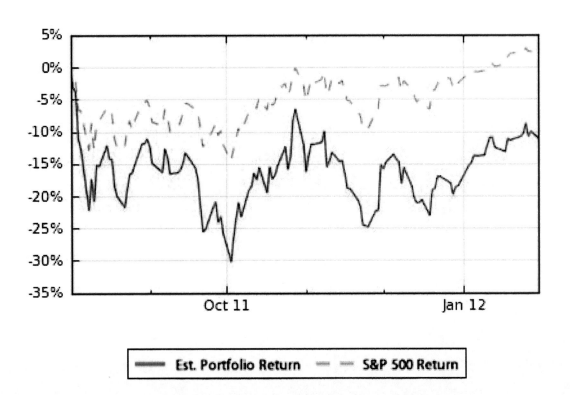

50

Scott Satterwhite - Artisan Funds

Scott Satterwhite - Artisan Funds

Company Name: **Artisan Partners Ltd. Partnership**
Portfolio Manager: **Scott Satterwhite, Mark Yockey**
Focus: **Small-Cap Value, International**

Artisan Partners LP has gained an fortunate reputation throughout the fund industry for two reasons. Firstly, their funds have posted strong results, and secondly, their funds are run by some of the best managers in the world. The correlation between these two is high especially in Artisan's case. The two most prominent funds Artisan offers are those focused on small-cap value and international offerings. The Milwaukee-based firm was founded in 1995 and over the last nine years has established itself as one of the best value and international stock pickers in the game.

Artisan's international fund picks stocks a little differently than most of our other fund families. This fund seeks non-domestic equities of all market capitalizations with a distinct focus on growth companies that possess efficient and effective management. Specifically, the fund looks for companies with sustainable growth opportunities (annual rate ranging 10%-30%), P/E's at a discount to current valuations, and a strong presence in their particular industries.

Morningstar's 1998 International Fund Manager of the Year, Mark L. Yockey is the person orchestrating the picks. Yockey, a managing director at Artisan, has been managing the international fund since its beginning in 1995, and has posted an annualized return of over 13%. He also manages Artisan's small-cap international fund, which as its name implies limits itself to smaller companies. While Yockey has the final say on what this fund invests in, he is not without a supporting cast. A team of six analysts accompany The Michigan State University MBA grad.

Another of Artisan's remarkable offerings is its small-cap value fund. Posting solid three-year, five-year and since-inception returns, the fund has developed a reputation as one of the best small-cap funds in the industry today. Scott Satterwhite and James Kieffer co-manage the fund. Both, holding the CFA designation, are former employees of the Wachovia Corporation, where their great stock picking relationship started.

Satterwhite has been at the controls of the small-cap value fund at Artisan since its 1997 inception, and Kieffer acted as his analyst for three years before being promoted to Satterwhite's stock picking peer and co-manager in 2000. The stock picking success of this team stems mainly from the two men's shared ideologies. There are four key components making up their small-cap value strategy. First on the list is looking for companies with the ability to significantly increase earnings in the future. The second component is not shunning under-analyzed companies. Third, finding companies with hidden assets, and finally, looking for companies with a recent change in new management, product line, or trend within the industry.

Based on the savvy management team and the indisputable track record of their top funds, Artisan is a great addition.

Based on the savvy management team and the indisputable track record of their top funds, Artisan is a great addition.

Company Name: Artisan Partners Partnership
Shares Held, Change in Shares, and Position Change as of February 1, 2012

Ticker	Mkt Cap	Div Yield	Share Value	Shares Held	Change in Shares
A	$14.8B	0.9%	$401.5M	7.9M shares	*decrease of 105.0K shares*
ACGL	$4.8B	-	$629.9M	19.7M shares	**increase of 504.5K shares**
ACN	$38.9B	2.4%	$400.6M	6.6M shares	*decrease of 103.9K shares*
ARW	$4.6B	-	$365.8M	8.8M shares	*decrease of 72.2K shares*
BIDU	$45.8B	-	$466.5M	3.3M shares	**increase of 198.7K shares**
CAM	$13.1B	-	$303.1M	6.0M shares	**increase of 410.1K shares**
CBE	$9.3B	1.9%	$340.9M	5.7M shares	*decrease of 87.0K shares*
CERN	$10.2B	-	$405.5M	6.6M shares	*decrease of 137.2K shares*
CP	$12.1B	1.7%	$496.9M	8.0M shares	**increase of 1.7M shares**
FOSL	$6.0B	-	$351.1M	3.0M shares	*decrease of 36.5K shares*
PCP	$24.0B	0.1%	$371.5M	2.3M shares	*decrease of 24.1K shares*
SIG	$4.0B	0.9%	$455.6M	9.7M shares	*decrease of 82.2K shares*
TEL	$14.5B	2.1%	$514.0M	14.0M shares	New Holding
TW	$4.4B	0.7%	$316.2M	4.8M shares	*decrease of 138.7K shares*
UL	$98.6B	3.8%	$346.8M	10.7M shares	**increase of 549.2K shares**

PORTFOLIO PERFORMANCE 6 MONTH

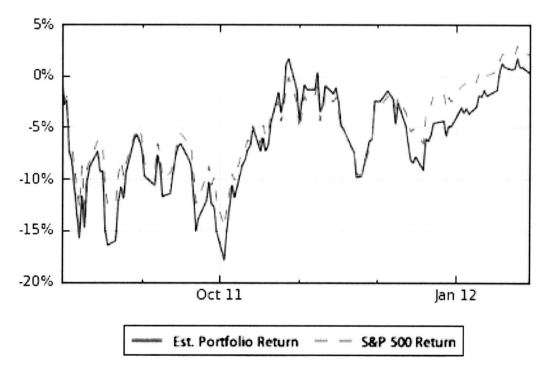

James Miles - Hotchkis and Wiley

James Miles - Hotchkis and Wiley

Company Name: **Hotchkis and Wiley Asset Management**
Portfolio Manager: **James Miles, David Green, and Stan Macher**
Focus: **Small and Mid Cap Value**

This value-based asset management company has spawned some of the best performing funds over the past 3 and 5 years, including its small- and mid-cap offerings. The focus is placed largely on proprietary research to pick great companies; research aimed at uncovering companies the market has wrongly undervalued. Year after year, this time-tested methodology of stock picking has proven itself at Hotchkis and Wiley. These managers seem to have perfected their process of selecting companies.

Each fund manager at Hotchkis is supported by an entourage of research analysts ensuring that each company invested in passes their stringent value-based requirements. These requirements include scrupulously examining both quantitative factors (such as earnings figures and ratios, including book value) and qualitative factors (such as tearing apart a company's business model to see if it's air tight). An additional factor in the success of Hotchkis is the willingness of its analysts to scour areas of the market that Wall Street or the market in general has temporarily ignored, in the hope of uncovering some investments that turn out to be diamonds in the rough.

Hotchkis' small- and mid-cap funds are led by three of the best money managers in the business. James Miles, who earned an MBA from UCLA accompanied by a MS from Stanford, co-manages both funds, while David Green, relying partially on his experience and analytical prowess gained as a member of the Goldman Sachs team, helps oversee the small-cap fund. The mid-cap fund is co-managed by Stan Macher. In a November 2003 Smart Money article, Macher described the style of investing at Hotchkis this way: "we're looking out at long-run earnings power, not the next month or quarter." Later, in a CNBC interview, he reiterated this idea, dismissing the notion of the fund selling a security in less than 6 to 12 months.

This attention to the long-term picture and long-term earnings potential instilled in all managers at Hotchkis separates them from a lot of the other firms. It demonstrates their willingness and patience to hold companies long enough for the market to properly value them.

The performance of this money management team, coupled with its stringent selection process and commitment to original research, makes Hotchkis and Wiley a firm that any astute investor should definitely watch.

Company Name: Hotchkis & Wiley Capital Management
Shares Held, Change in Shares, and Position Change as of February 1, 2012

Ticker	Mkt Cap	Div Yield	Share Value	Shares Held	Change in Shares
ALL	$14.6B	2.9%	$487.6M	20.6M shares	**increase of 4.6M shares**
CA	$12.1B	3.9%	$395.7M	20.4M shares	*decrease of 2.2M shares*
CMCSK	$	1.8%	$290.7M	14.0M shares	**increase of 614.3K shares**
COP	$92.1B	3.8%	$388.3M	6.1M shares	*decrease of 1.2M shares*
EXC	$26.2B	5.3%	$398.0M	9.3M shares	*decrease of 2.1M shares*
GPS	$9.2B	2.4%	$302.5M	18.6M shares	**increase of 4.6M shares**
HPQ	$55.5B	1.7%	$501.3M	22.3M shares	**increase of 4.0M shares**
JCP	$8.8B	1.9%	$302.3M	11.3M shares	**increase of 548.5K shares**
JPM	$79.9B	2.7%	$463.6M	15.4M shares	**increase of 1.4M shares**
LMT	$26.5B	4.9%	$357.7M	4.9M shares	*decrease of 778.6K shares*
MSFT	$245.0B	2.7%	$300.5M	12.1M shares	*decrease of 3.2M shares*
PEG	$15.3B	4.5%	$333.0M	10.0M shares	*decrease of 679.4K shares*
RDS.B	$	4.6%	$376.2M	6.1M shares	*decrease of 2.2M shares*
VOD	$136.1B	5.3%	$356.9M	13.9M shares	*decrease of 3.6M shares*
WFC	$156.0B	1.6%	$462.3M	19.2M shares	*decrease of 949.4K shares*

PORTFOLIO PERFORMANCE 6 MONTH

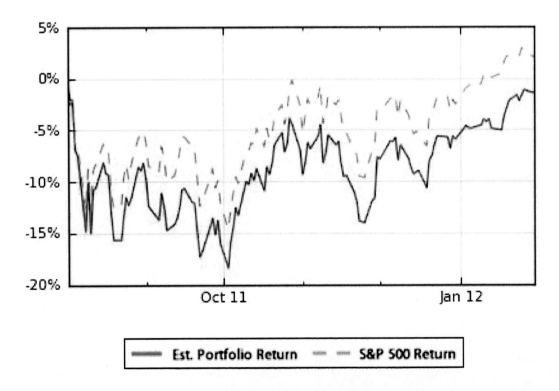

John Keeley - Keeley Asset Management

John Keeley - Keeley Asset Management

Company Name: **Keeley Asset Management**
Portfolio Manager: **John L. Keeley, Jr.**
Focus: **Small-Cap Value, Mid-Cap Value**

John Keeley Jr., manager of Keeley's small- and mid-cap funds, has quietly become one of the best money managers in the business. Through a strict investment discipline focused on identifying undervalued companies with solid financials and a history of earnings growth, Keeley's main small-cap fund has consistently trumped market returns since its inception in 1993.

Like all of our managers, Keeley has a proven track record backed by relevant education and extensive experience in the financial industry. Keeley has earned a master's in business administration from the University of Chicago along with the Chartered Financial Analyst designation. More importantly, John Keeley Jr. having started his career as a financial analyst with Standard Oil in 1966 has been in the investment industry for more than 40 years. After working for several other firms in the industry, Keeley started his own, starting Keeley Investment Corp., a broker-dealer, in 1977.

The investment strategy of both the small-cap (less than $1.5 billion) and mid-cap ($1.5 billion to $5 billion) value funds are the same. The emphasis is placed on finding companies that have been ignored by the market. This strategy focuses on companies that are going through corporate redevelopment or trading at low valuations, including spin-offs, companies emerging from bankruptcy, and companies trading below intrinsic value. The strategy does not just bet on turnarounds - there is also a strict focus on financials, cash flow generation, balance sheet strength and growth.

Together with the fund's strong discipline, this market-beating strategy is the main reason that we feel Keeley Asset Management is a great addition. This is only further solidified by John Keeley Jr.'s large personal investment in the funds he manages, not to mention the five-star rating the fund received from Morningstar. This is definitely a manager to watch closely.

Company Name: Keeley Asset Management
Shares Held, Change in Shares, and Position Change as of February 1, 2012

Ticker	Mkt Cap	Div Yield	Share Value	Shares Held	Change in Shares
BND	$	3.1%	$169.7M	2.0M shares	New Holding
BR	$2.9B	2.7%	$50.9M	2.5M shares	*decrease of 94.1K shares*
CBI	$4.3B	0.5%	$49.9M	1.7M shares	*decrease of 222.9K shares*
DEL	$862.8M	0.4%	$51.3M	860.0K shares	*decrease of 32.9K shares*
FLO	$2.6B	3.1%	$49.8M	2.6M shares	*decrease of 217.6K shares*
GWR	$2.6B	-	$45.1M	969.6K shares	*decrease of 120.5K shares*
HRC	$2.0B	1.4%	$46.0M	1.5M shares	*decrease of 66.6K shares*
ITC	$3.7B	1.9%	$61.7M	796.2K shares	*decrease of 72.9K shares*
KSU	$7.5B	-	$56.0M	1.1M shares	*decrease of 113.7K shares*
MTN	$1.5B	1.4%	$47.5M	1.3M shares	*decrease of 60.8K shares*
SBH	$3.8B	-	$51.2M	3.1M shares	*decrease of 991.9K shares*
THS	$2.0B	-	$56.3M	909.9K shares	*decrease of 75.0K shares*
WAB	$3.4B	0.2%	$57.5M	1.1M shares	*decrease of 220.2K shares*
WXS	$2.2B	-	$50.7M	1.3M shares	*decrease of 78.8K shares*
WYN	$6.1B	1.5%	$54.5M	1.9M shares	*decrease of 82.4K shares*

PORTFOLIO PERFORMANCE 6 MONTH

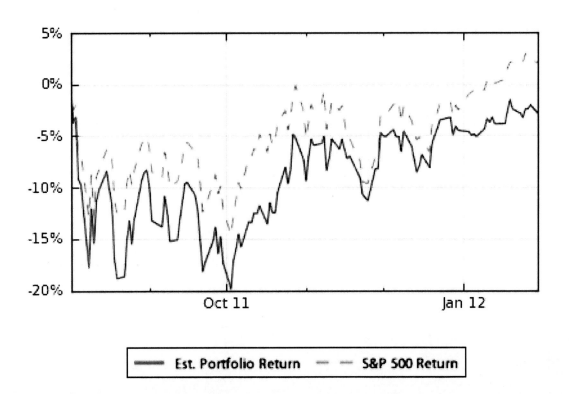

William B. Frels - Mairs & Power Funds

William B. Frels - Mairs & Power Funds

Company Name: **Mairs and Power Funds**
Portfolio Manager: **William B. Frels**
Focus: **Large Blend**

Many people in the investment community claim to be proponents of long-term investing where the focus is buying companies and not stocks. However, there are very few that actually follow through on this strategy. Mairs & Power is one investment company that epitomizes this tough-to-follow philosophy. This small firm currently holds many positions that have been in its funds for nearly ten years. They focus on a conservative growth approach in its investments, looking for companies with a large growth potential at a reasonable valuation. This strict investment philosophy, and the company's strong dedication to upholding it, is what has produced market-beating returns.

Founded in 1958, Mairs & Power Growth Fund is headed by William Frels who took over as head portfolio manager in 2004 after George Mairs III retired. Having been with the firm since 1992,Frels, has co-managed the growth fund since 2000 and is also the lead manager for the company's balanced fund. Frels has a bachelor's degree in finance from the University of Wisconsin, along with a Chartered Financial Analyst designation.

The investment strategy used by Mairs & Power is focused on looking for growing companies with fair valuations, but is inclusive only of companies the firm knows and understands. This Buffett-like thinking has led to a strong focus on Midwestern firms, where Mairs & Power operates, due to the idea that they have a greater ability to fully understand the companies within their own region. While this does limit the companies that can be added to the fund, this is not a major problem for a company that limits its holdings to fewer than 50.

Both funds under Mairs & Power management have been given a five star rating by Morningstar. As noted by the fund rating agency, Mairs & Power's provides strong stewardship and performance coupled with below-average expenses for investors. In fact, the company tops not only the market, but its peers as well.

This strong investment philosophy and management team, along with the firm's long history, is good reason to follow the moves of Mairs & Power closely.

Company Name: Mairs & Power INC
Shares Held, Change in Shares, and Position Change as of February 1, 2012

Ticker	Mkt Cap	Div Yield	Share Value	Shares Held	Change in Shares
BAX	$31.4B	2.4%	$96.8M	1.7M shares	**increase of 6.5K shares**
BMS	$3.2B	3.0%	$98.0M	3.3M shares	**increase of 42.4K shares**
DCI	$5.3B	0.9%	$112.0M	2.0M shares	*decrease of 20.3K shares*
ECL	$14.0B	1.3%	$119.0M	2.4M shares	*decrease of 28.2K shares*
EMR	$38.1B	3.1%	$112.1M	2.7M shares	**increase of 142.6K shares**
GGG	$2.6B	2.0%	$99.0M	2.9M shares	*decrease of 36.8K shares*
GIS	$25.8B	3.1%	$98.6M	2.6M shares	*decrease of 138.3K shares*
HON	$45.0B	2.6%	$104.4M	2.4M shares	**increase of 32.8K shares**
JNJ	$179.1B	3.5%	$109.7M	1.7M shares	*decrease of 41.7K shares*
MDT	$41.4B	2.5%	$121.6M	3.7M shares	**increase of 39.9K shares**
MMM	$61.2B	2.5%	$148.7M	2.1M shares	**increase of 34.7K shares**
PNR	$3.6B	2.4%	$107.2M	3.3M shares	**increase of 24.0K shares**
TGT	$33.6B	2.4%	$134.1M	2.7M shares	**increase of 36.2K shares**
USB	$53.2B	1.8%	$104.2M	4.4M shares	**increase of 48.7K shares**
VAL	$4.0B	1.9%	$112.1M	3.6M shares	**increase of 104.7K shares**

PORTFOLIO PERFORMANCE 6 MONTH

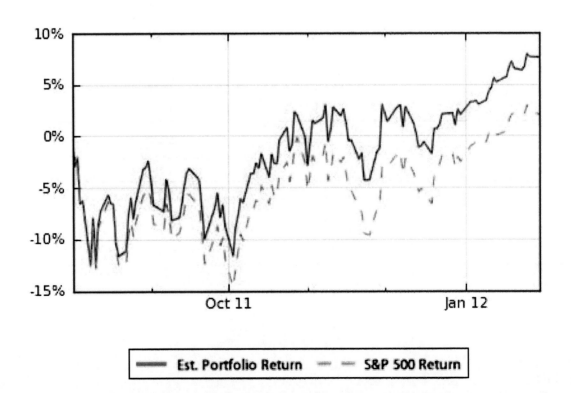

Bill & Melinda Gates Foundation

Bill & Melinda Gates Foundation

The foundation works to reduce inequities around the world. In the developing world, it focuses on improving health and alleviating extreme poverty. In the United States, the foundation supports programs related to education. In its local region, the foundation promotes strategies and programs that help low income families. The foundation is based in Seattle, Washington, with branch offices in Washington, D.C., New Delhi, India, Beijing, China and London, United Kingdom. Its Trustees are Bill and Melinda Gates, and Warren Buffett

The trust holds the donated investment assets from Bill and Melinda Gates, and receives contributions from Warren Buffett. The primary role of the trust is to manage the investment assets and transfer proceeds to the foundation as necessary to achieve the foundation's charitable goals. Its trustees are Bill and Melinda Gates.

About the Bill & Melinda Gates Foundation Asset Trust

In October 2006, our trustees created a two-entity structure. One entity, the Bill & Melinda Gates Foundation, distributes money to grantees. The other, the Bill & Melinda Gates Foundation Asset Trust, manages the endowment assets. This structure enables us to separate our program work from the investment of our assets.

How the asset trust works

The asset trust holds the endowment, including the annual installments of Warren Buffett's gift, and funds the foundation. Bill and Melinda are the trustees for the asset trust, and the endowment continues to be managed, as it has been for more than 10 years, by a team of outside investment managers.

The role of the foundation

The foundation conducts all operations and grantmaking work and is the entity from which all grants are made. Bill, Melinda, and Warren are the trustees for the foundation. Warren has no involvement in the investment of the endowment through the asset trust, including decisions that might be made regarding Berkshire Hathaway Inc. stock.

Because Bill, Melinda, and Warren believe the right approach is to focus the foundation's work in the 21st century, we will spend all of our resources within 50 years after Bill's and Melinda's deaths. In addition, Warren has stipulated that the proceeds from the Berkshire Hathaway shares he still owns upon his death are to be used for philanthropic purposes within 10 years after his estate has been settled.

The decision to use all of the foundation's resources in this century underscores our optimism for progress and determination to do as much as possible, as soon as possible, to address the comparatively narrow set of issues we've chosen to focus on.

Program-Related Investments: Leveraging Our Resources to Catalyze Broader Support for Our Mission

As the global financial crisis puts a strain on all sectors—and adversely affects those most in need—we must look for opportunities to maximize the impact that our funds and partners can have in advancing our mission and core issues.

Through tools like low-interest loans, guaranties, and equity investments, the foundation will apply some of its resources to support companies, investment funds, financial institutions and other revenue-generating enterprises that further the foundation's charitable purpose. Program-related investments (PRIs) can be important tools for the foundation to stimulate private-sector driven innovation, to encourage market-driven efficiencies, and to attract external capital to the foundation's priority initiatives.

Bill & Melinda Gates Foundation FAQ

Q. What is the foundation's new approach to Program-Related Investments?

A. We are working with a range of partners to use PRIs to deepen the impact of our work. We believe that investments are useful tools for situations in which our program strategies are best served by partnering with revenue-generating enterprises, such as companies, investment funds, financial institutions and NGOs. These entities may not be able to access investment capital from the private markets because the markets or entities that serve the poor may be perceived as too risky or costly to serve, or investors don't have good information to assess the opportunities. By providing investment capital directly or by reducing risk to investors, we can help our partners access the capital they need to grow and demonstrate to the market that financially viable opportunities exist that serve the needs of poor or otherwise disadvantaged persons. We know we can't solve all problems with these types of investments – grant-making remains critical for those sectors that have a low likelihood of generating sufficient revenues or be addressed by market forces. We have established an initial program with an envelope of $400 million to invest in a range of opportunities. The capital for PRI investments or guarantees will be provided by this special $400M pool which will be managed by the CFO's office of the foundation. Out of this pool, we will invest in PRIs that directly and meaningfully contribute to the achievement of the foundation's charitable purposes.

Q. What types of investments will the foundation do?

A. We will evaluate a full range of investment opportunities that could include:

• Debt instruments such as loans to NGOs, financial institutions or companies;

• Equity instruments investments in funds or purchases of shares in companies;

• Guaranty instruments such as bond back-stops or credit guaranties.

• Any PRI opportunity must closely align with our program strategies, for example: increasing financing for agricultural smallholders in Africa, supporting charter school facilities expansion, or increasing investment in global health technologies.

Q. What criteria will the foundation use to evaluate investments?

A. We have only a limited pool of investment capital so we want to be careful how we use it. We will evaluate investments according to three core criteria:

Strong alignment with our program strategies: We will do PRIs that directly support our program strategies and contribute (via measurable outcomes and impacts) to our program goals;

High leverage of external capital: We expect our investment to be at a minimum matched by other investors (a 1:1 leverage) but would like to see our capital mobilize other capital at a 5:1 ratio.

Transformative investments: We are looking for investments that promote sustainable, scalable solutions that can demonstrate to the market that good opportunities exist for serving poor or otherwise disadvantaged persons. We are also looking for investments in which our capital makes a difference in getting the deal done and increasing the focus on the poor.

Q. What types of organizations will be partners?

A. Because leveraging external capital is such an important part of this work, we are actively seeking partners to co-invest. These types of partners could include other private investors, or investors with a commitment to social goals. We could also partner with other philanthropies, government entities and public finance institutions, especially development finance institutions such as the World Bank.

Q. How will the foundation determine which organizations to invest in?

A. As with all our work, foundation staff will identify the right partners and organizations to receive program-related investments. All investments will be closely aligned with program strategies and will be managed by a team with specialized expertise in investment structuring in coordination with the program teams.

Q. How is MRI (mission-related investing) or SRI (Socially Responsible Investing) different from what the foundation is doing?

A. All of our PRIs will have as their primary purpose the achievement of specific charitable objectives that are aligned with the foundation's mission, and no significant purpose of the investments will be to generate income or an appreciation of capital. In contrast, the primary purpose of Mission Related Investing and Socially Responsible Investing is to generate a return on capital, while investing in profitable ventures that also have a social purpose.

Q. Who will manage these funds – the foundation or the investment managers overseeing the endowment?

A. These funds will be managed by a specialized team working under the CFO of the foundation in coordination with the program and legal teams. Since we are a program driven organization, it's critical to continue to work with program teams to ensure that all of our investments are aligned with program strategies.

Q. Is this a risky approach for the foundation?

A. Yes, there is some risk involved. We are positioned to take some risk and believe this is an important role for the sector—seeding new ideas, sharing lessons learned, and bringing new partners to table to advance some of the most promising innovations for the benefit of those most in need.

To ensure that we continue to advance our ambitious program goals, helping all people no matter where they live lead a healthy and productive life, the foundation must think creatively about how to extend the reach of our resources. Especially as the global financial crisis puts a strain on all sectors—and adversely affects those most in need—we must look for opportunities to maximize the impact that our funds and partners can have in advancing our mission and core issues.

Q. What happens if or when these investments earn a profit?

A. All of our PRIs will have as their primary purpose the achievement of specific charitable objectives that are aligned with the foundation's mission, and no significant purpose of the investments will be to generate income or an appreciation of capital. In the case where an investment does earn a profit, the funds are returned to the foundation and utilized either for investment in additional PRIs or for traditional grant-making.

Q. What happens to any intellectual property (IP) associated with an investment?

A. As in our grant-making, the ownership of patents and other IP associated with an investment is retained by the company or entity that develops the IP. However, many of our PRIs include global access rights that ensure that promising technologies are developed for the purpose of serving the poor or saving lives, which may involve the creative management of IP rights that balances the foundation's charitable objectives with the needs of our business partners.

Company Name: Bill & Melinda Gates Foundation
Shares Held, Change in Shares, and Position Change as of February 1, 2012

Ticker	Mkt Cap	Div Yield	Share Value	Shares Held	Change in Shares
AN	$5.1B	-	$353.8M	10.8M shares	No Change
BP	$138.0B	3.8%	$257.3M	7.1M shares	No Change
BRK.B	$186.5B	-	$6.8B	96.2M shares	**increase of 14.3M shares**
CAT	$71.9B	1.7%	$745.1M	10.1M shares	**increase of 500.0K shares**
CCI	$13.8B	-	$216.9M	5.3M shares	No Change
CNI	$33.6B	2.0%	$570.2M	8.6M shares	No Change
COST	$35.3B	1.2%	$503.3M	6.1M shares	No Change
ECL	$14.0B	1.3%	$213.5M	4.4M shares	No Change
KO	$153.1B	2.8%	$789.2M	11.7M shares	No Change
KOF	$18.1B	2.1%	$551.4M	6.2M shares	No Change
MCD	$100.9B	2.8%	$867.0M	9.9M shares	No Change
TV	$11.2B	0.7%	$310.4M	16.9M shares	No Change
WM	$16.0B	3.9%	$606.7M	18.6M shares	No Change
WMT	$208.6B	2.4%	$506.2M	9.8M shares	No Change
XOM	$411.4B	2.2%	$555.2M	7.6M shares	No Change

PORTFOLIO PERFORMANCE 6 MONTH

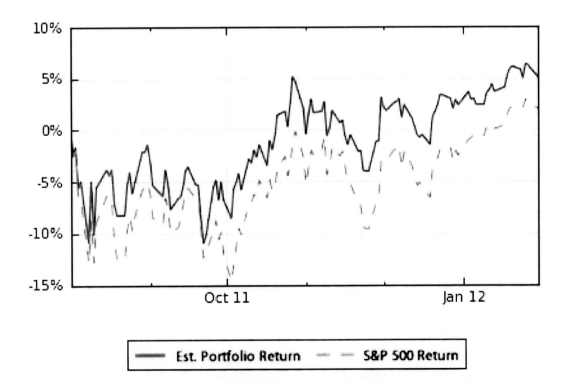

84

Charles Schwab Trust Company,
A Division Of Charles Schwab Bank

Charles Schwab Trust Company, A Division Of Charles Schwab Bank

The Charles Schwab Corporation has been a leader in financial services for more than three decades. Through advocacy and innovation, the company has worked to make investing more affordable, more accessible and more understandable to all.

Today, Schwab meets the needs of individual and institutional clients through two operating segments:

Investor Services provides retail brokerage and banking operations to millions of individuals.

Institutional Services meets "business-to-business" needs through Advisor Services, Retirement Plan Services, Corporate Brokerage Services and Retirement Business Services.

Financial Highlights

The Charles Schwab Corporation has reported results for fourth quarter 2010.

Consolidated Financial Results	3 Months Ended Dec. 31, 2010	3 Months Ended Dec. 31, 2009
Net revenues *(in millions)*	$1,127	$986
Net Income *(in millions)*	$119	$164
Diluted earnings per share	$0.10	$0.14
Pre-tax profit margin	20.3%	27.0%
Return on stockholders' equity *(annualized)*	8%	13%
Client Assets & Accounts		
Total client assets	$1.57 trillion	$1.42 trillion
Active brokerage accounts	7.9 million	7.7 million
Corporate retirement plan participants	1.47 million	1.46 million
Banking accounts	690,000	567,000

Schwab Facts

Employees: 12,800 full-time employees

Executive Management: Founder and Chairman Charles Schwab; President and Chief Executive Officer Walt Bettinger

History: Charles Schwab and Co., Inc., was launched in 1973, and the company began offering discount brokerage on May 1, 1975.

Locations: Headquartered in San Francisco, Schwab operates 302 domestic branch offices in 45 states, one branch in Puerto Rico and one branch in London. Hong Kong clients are served through a Schwab subsidiary.

Social Responsibility: Charles Schwab Foundation makes average annual contributions averaging $4 million to more than 2,300 nonprofit organizations.

Other Products and Services: Schwab also serves individuals through banking, mutual funds and other financial products and services.

Company Name: Charles Schwab Trust Company, A Division Of Charles Schwab Bank
Shares Held, Change in Shares, and Position Change as of February 1, 2012

Ticker	Mkt Cap	Div Yield	Share Value	Shares Held	Change in Shares
AAPL	$416.9B	-	$661.5M	1.7M shares	increase of 163.7K shares
CVX	$207.0B	3.1%	$476.6M	5.1M shares	increase of 832.5K shares
GE	$200.9B	3.6%	$360.9M	23.7M shares	increase of 207.8K shares
IBM	$224.4B	1.6%	$556.3M	3.2M shares	*decrease of 130.0K shares*
JNJ	$179.1B	3.5%	$345.2M	5.4M shares	increase of 64.2K shares
JPM	$79.9B	2.7%	$343.8M	11.4M shares	increase of 184.6K shares
KO	$153.1B	2.8%	$249.9M	3.7M shares	increase of 27.3K shares
MSFT	$245.0B	2.7%	$341.2M	13.7M shares	increase of 107.4K shares
ORCL	$143.0B	0.8%	$252.3M	8.8M shares	increase of 1.4K shares
PFE	$165.1B	4.1%	$314.9M	17.8M shares	increase of 155.4K shares
PG	$176.9B	3.3%	$294.8M	4.7M shares	increase of 24.8K shares
T	$172.7B	6.0%	$398.5M	14.0M shares	increase of 343.0K shares
VZ	$105.3B	5.3%	$333.5M	9.1M shares	increase of 895.2K shares
WFC	$156.0B	1.6%	$340.6M	14.1M shares	increase of 79.0K shares
XOM	$411.4B	2.2%	$663.2M	9.1M shares	increase of 143.5K shares

PORTFOLIO PERFORMANCE 6 MONTH

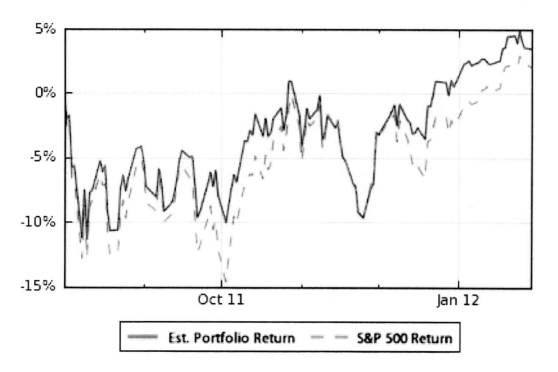

Citadel Investment Group

Citadel Investment Group

Citadel LLC (formerly known as Citadel Investment Group, L.L.C.) is a global financial institution based in Chicago, Illinois. Founded in 1990 by trader Kenneth C. Griffin, the firm today deploys investment capital across multiple asset classes and strategies. Current activities include equity options market-making, hedge fund administration, investment banking advisory, and a fund of funds business that deploys capital with unaffiliated managers.

Citadel deploys capital through multiple investment strategies across the world's major markets.

Equities

Equities combines detailed, fundamental stock selection with a rigorous portfolio construction and risk management framework. Equities seeks to be Beta-neutral (i.e., non-correlated with investments in stock market indices) on a daily basis, and primarily invests in liquid equity markets. The investment process is driven by detailed, bottom-up company analysis. Equities seeks to generate alpha by identifying out- and under-performing stocks in each sector team's universe. The group is organized into seven industry sector groups: Communications, Media and Entertainment; Consumer; Energy and Utilities; Financials; Healthcare; Industrials; and Technology.

Convertibles

The Convertibles strategy applies a differentiated approach that combines inputs from Citadel's proprietary capital structure model with fundamental insights. It yields a diversified portfolio, composed primarily of U.S. and European holdings, that is backed by the firm's deep experience in managing convertibles through multiple market cycles.

Energy

Energy encompasses Citadel's activities in the North American natural gas market and European gas and power markets, as well as its activities in the global crude oil and refined products markets. The Energy team combines fundamental market expertise with quantitative analytics to identify directional and relative value investment opportunities.

Macro

Macro deploys capital across global macro themes informed by macro-analysis and technical perspectives. These themes are expressed through directional and relative value investment strategies primarily across G20 and liquid emerging markets, fixed income, currency and equity securities and commodity markets. The team leverages fundamental analysis and quantitative models through a dynamic and disciplined approach.

Rates

Rates invests primarily in liquid fixed-income products, mainly in G10 countries, either through direct investments in government bonds and agency mortgage-backed securities or through derivatives such as interest-rate swaps, futures, options, repurchase agreements, and reverse repurchase agreements.

Fundamental Credit

The Fundamental Credit strategy combines detailed fundamental research and quantitative portfolio analysis to invest primarily in single-name credit instruments in a beta-neutral, relative value framework. Fundamental Credit is organized by industry sector groups and seeks to maximize alpha by isolating idiosyncratic credit movement based on underlying issuer-specific credit fundamentals and catalysts.

Quantitative Credit

Quantitative Credit deploys capital through two main strategies: Credit Arbitrage and Structured Credit. Credit Arbitrage is a relative value strategy designed to capture value primarily based on the potential differences in value between bonds and CDS and fixed income indices and their constituent parts. Structured Credit focuses on tactical trading opportunities across fixed income index tranches.

Mortgages

Mortgages primarily invest in a broad range of non-agency residential mortgage-backed securities (RMBS), whole loans and related financial instruments within the mortgage asset class. Strategies are developed by rigorous fundamental research and analytics and supported by proprietary modeling, trading tools and information management infrastructure.

Company Name: Citadel Investment Group
Shares Held, Change in Shares, and Position Change as of February 1, 2012

Ticker	Mkt Cap	Div Yield	Share Value	Shares Held	Change in Shares
AAPL	$416.9B	-	$928.1M	2.4M shares	**increase of 1.6M shares**
AMTD	$9.0B	1.5%	$158.1M	10.8M shares	**increase of 5.5M shares**
APC	$39.4B	0.4%	$165.3M	2.6M shares	**increase of 880.8K shares**
C	$90.2B	0.1%	$157.3M	6.1M shares	**increase of 1.7M shares**
CMA	$5.5B	1.4%	$159.6M	6.9M shares	**increase of 5.0M shares**
CMCSA	$71.7B	1.7%	$155.8M	7.4M shares	**increase of 2.6M shares**
CME	$15.9B	2.3%	$132.0M	535.7K shares	**increase of 92.1K shares**
COG	$6.8B	0.2%	$179.6M	2.9M shares	**increase of 730.2K shares**
ETFC	$2.3B	-	$249.8M	27.4M shares	No Change
FITB	$12.1B	2.5%	$133.8M	13.2M shares	**increase of 10.9M shares**
GOOG	$187.7B	-	$188.1M	365.2K shares	**increase of 187.9K shares**
IVZ	$10.3B	2.2%	$177.4M	11.4M shares	**increase of 7.5M shares**
NDAQ	$4.6B	-	$132.9M	5.7M shares	**increase of 4.2M shares**
PNC	$31.0B	2.4%	$199.4M	4.1M shares	**increase of 445.2K shares**
XOM	$411.4B	2.2%	$149.6M	2.1M shares	**increase of 2.0M shares**

PORTFOLIO PERFORMANCE 6 MONTH

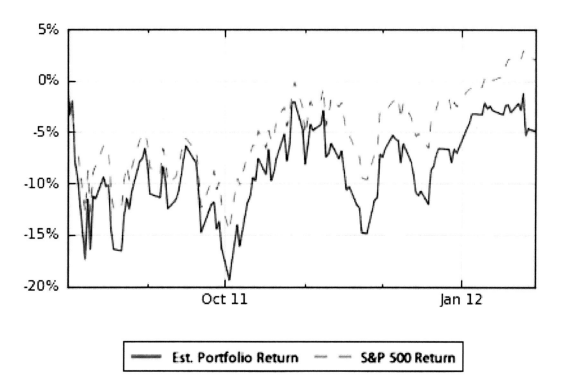

Friedberg Investment Management

Friedberg Investment Management

Friedberg Investment Management (FIM) is an independent, fee-based, money management firm, not affiliated with any brokerage firm, mutual fund organization, financial planning firm or insurance company, and do not charge commissions.

Investment management is not so much the management of money as it is the management of risk. Most investors take either too much risk or too little. FIM, believe the challenge is to invest each client's dollars to obtain the highest possible return commensurate with the degree of risk each client is willing and able to assume. For some clients, this means seeking long term growth in the stock market. For others, it means earning substantial interest or dividend income, ideally rising over time, without significant risk to principal.

How Does FIM Operate?

FIM manages each portfolio separately--there is no comingling or pooling of funds. FIM does not take custody of a client's funds or securities. Simply establish accounts at fully insured brokerage firms which offer our clients low commissions, and they manage these accounts through limited power-of-attorney. They issue a statement every month showing profit or loss as well as holdings.

Client Relationships

Unlike a mutual fund, each investor has direct access to the individuals at FIM who manage their portfolios. And unlike a brokerage firm, the principals of FIM are decision makers, not order takers. Portfolios are thus very closely tailored to the needs of each investor.

Who Are FIM's Clients?

Primarily individuals and small retirement plans. FIM can manage IRAs, Roths, individual 401-ks, SEPs, trusts and custodial accounts that are oriented to each investor's preference. They manage growth and balanced portfolios for investors seeking appreciation and income generating portfolios for investors desiring income.

How Did FIM Originate?

Jeffrey L. Friedberg was raised in a small coal-mining town in eastern Pennsylvania. He graduated first in his high school class, earned Dean's List while at MIT and was awarded a graduate Fellowship at Caltech. Although his degrees were in Geology and Geophysics, Friedberg became actively involved in the stock market while pursuing a rewarding career in Geophysics. In 1979, Friedberg decided to become registered and licensed as an Investment Advisor in order to invest other people's money as he was investing his own. He thus founded FIM, in effect transforming an enjoyable sideline into a successful business endeavor.

Company Name: Friedberg Investment Management
Shares Held, Change in Shares, and Position Change as of February 1, 2012

Ticker	Mkt Cap	Div Yield	Share Value	Shares Held	Change in Shares
AMT	$24.7B	-	$3.0M	55.7K shares	**increase of 940 shares**
ANSS	$5.6B	-	$4.7M	96.2K shares	*decrease of 5.2K shares*
CLH	$3.4B	-	$2.9M	56.5K shares	*decrease of 1.6K shares*
CRR	$2.3B	1.0%	$3.1M	30.1K shares	*decrease of 1.4K shares*
DLR	$7.2B	3.9%	$5.3M	96.4K shares	*decrease of 1.1K shares*
EQT	$7.2B	1.8%	$5.8M	108.1K shares	*decrease of 1.9K shares*
ESL	$1.9B	-	$5.0M	96.1K shares	**increase of 1.1K shares**
FLIR	$4.0B	0.9%	$2.9M	116.1K shares	*decrease of 12.5K shares*
IDXX	$4.6B	-	$5.3M	77.5K shares	*decrease of 2.7K shares*
INT	$3.2B	0.3%	$4.1M	125.0K shares	*decrease of 8.2K shares*
ISRG	$17.9B	-	$3.8M	10.4K shares	*decrease of 789 shares*
NATI	$3.2B	1.5%	$5.1M	223.0K shares	*decrease of 5.4K shares*
OIS	$4.1B	-	$3.4M	66.9K shares	**increase of 6.5K shares**
PAA	$11.4B	5.3%	$5.3M	90.2K shares	**increase of 5.2K shares**
SDRL	$17.2B	8.2%	$2.7M	97.9K shares	**increase of 970 shares**

PORTFOLIO PERFORMANCE 6 MONTH

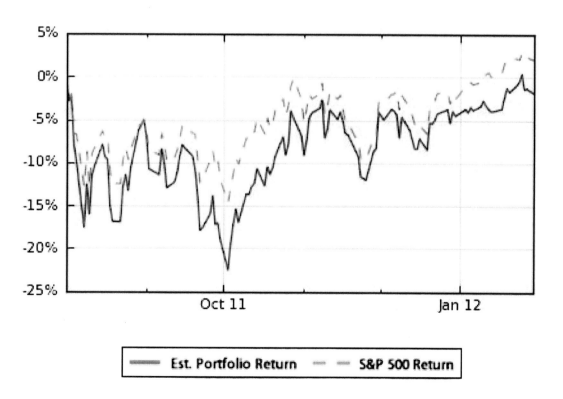

Legend: —— Est. Portfolio Return   – – S&P 500 Return

Goldman Sachs

Goldman Sachs

Goldman Sachs is a global investment banking and securities firm which engages in investment banking, securities, investment management, and other financial services primarily with institutional clients. Goldman Sachs was founded in 1869 and is headquartered at 200 West Street in the Lower Manhattan area of New York City, with additional offices in major international financial centers. The firm provides mergers and acquisitions advice, underwriting services, asset management, and prime brokerage to its clients, which include corporations, governments and individuals. The firm also engages in proprietary trading and private equity deals, and is a primary dealer in the United States Treasury security market.

Former employees include Robert Rubin and Henry Paulson who served as United States Secretary of the Treasury under Presidents Bill Clinton and George W. Bush, respectively.

Goldman Sachs:

• Advise companies on buying and selling businesses, help them manage risks and raise capital, which enables them to grow, launch new products, build factories and invest in research and development.

• Help local, state and national governments finance their operations. This enables governments and communities to make infrastructure improvements, like roads and bridges, hospitals and schools.

• Buy and sell equities, bonds, currencies and commodities to facilitate transactions by clients in all of the key financial markets. This helps businesses of all sizes find the capital they need to help create jobs and fuel growth.

• Connect buyers and sellers, linking investors with businesses and governments in need of capital.

• Help ensure that markets are efficient and liquid, so investors and companies can meet their needs, whether to invest, raise money or manage risk.

• Manage assets for institutions, including mutual funds, pension funds and foundations, as well as individuals, in the form of retirement plans, to help them preserve and increase financial security.

• Invest our capital, together with clients' capital, in growing businesses, which helps create jobs.

Company Name: Goldman Sachs
Shares Held, Change in Shares, and Position Change as of February 1, 2012

Ticker	Mkt Cap	Div Yield	Share Value	Shares Held	Change in Shares
AAPL	$416.9B	-	$2.5B	6.5M shares	**increase of 402.2K shares**
DG	$14.4B	-	$1.8B	46.4M shares	*decrease of 6.1M shares*
EFA	$	3.3%	$1.1B	22.7M shares	**increase of 339.2K shares**
EWZ	$	2.3%	$1.3B	24.5M shares	**increase of 13.1M shares**
GE	$200.9B	3.6%	$1.1B	70.8M shares	*decrease of 990.6K shares*
GOOG	$187.7B	-	$1.4B	2.8M shares	*decrease of 124.6K shares*
IWM	$	1.3%	$3.3B	51.0M shares	**increase of 3.5M shares**
JPM	$79.9B	2.7%	$866.9M	28.8M shares	*decrease of 61.3K shares*
MSFT	$245.0B	2.7%	$1.3B	51.8M shares	*decrease of 3.9M shares*
ORCL	$143.0B	0.8%	$966.8M	33.6M shares	*decrease of 1.8M shares*
PEP	$102.8B	3.1%	$1.0B	16.9M shares	*decrease of 5.2M shares*
QCOM	$97.5B	1.5%	$1.1B	21.7M shares	*decrease of 1.8M shares*
SPY	$	2.0%	$8.8B	78.0M shares	**increase of 26.2M shares**
VWO	$	2.2%	$993.8M	27.7M shares	*decrease of 224.3K shares*
XOM	$411.4B	2.2%	$1.1B	15.2M shares	**increase of 3.4M shares**

PORTFOLIO PERFORMANCE 6 MONTH

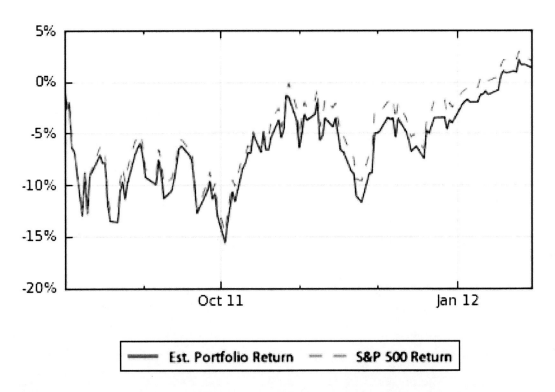

Paulson & Co

Paulson & Co

Paulson Advantage fund returned 38% in 2008, 13.8% in 2009 and 21% in 2010 net of fees. New York native earned M.B.A. at Harvard. Worked at Odyssey Partners, then Bear Stearns. Launched Paulson & Co. in 1994. Started exploiting perceived real estate bubble by devising debt trades, betting against ABX (mortgage) index in 2006. Personally pocketed $3.5 billion shorting subprime in 2007; Credit Opportunities fund soared 590% net of fees that year. Now betting on gold, banks. Largest public holdings in December: Bank of America, Citigroup, AngloGold Ashanti. Assets: $32 billion.

Became a billionaire in 2007 shorting subprime securities and earning a $3.5 billion payout.

Early life

John Paulson was born in Queens, New York, the son of Jacqueline and Alfredo Paulson, a Chief Financial Officer for Ruder Finn. Paulson attended the Whitestone Hebrew Centre (a United Synagogue of Conservative Judaism school) in Whitestone.

He earned his bachelor's degree in finance from New York University's College of Business and Public Administration (now called NYU Leonard N. Stern School of Business), where he graduated first in his class. He earned his MBA from Harvard Business School.

Company Name: Paulson & Co
Shares Held, Change in Shares, and Position Change as of February 1, 2012

Ticker	Mkt Cap	Div Yield	Share Value	Shares Held	Change in Shares
APC	$39.4B	0.4%	$893.5M	14.2M shares	*decrease of 2.5M shares*
AU	$17.6B	0.7%	$1.5B	36.7M shares	*decrease of 3.2M shares*
BAC	$73.8B	0.6%	$393.6M	64.3M shares	**increase of 3.9M shares**
C	$90.2B	0.1%	$643.1M	25.1M shares	*decrease of 8.4M shares*
COF	$21.1B	0.4%	$879.8M	22.2M shares	**increase of 1.1M shares**
GFI	$12.2B	1.4%	$376.3M	24.6M shares	*decrease of 136.3K shares*
GLD	$	-	$3.2B	20.3M shares	*decrease of 11.2M shares*
HIG	$7.8B	2.3%	$627.1M	38.9M shares	*decrease of 1.7M shares*
MGM	$6.4B	-	$378.5M	40.7M shares	*decrease of 960.5K shares*
MYL	$8.9B	-	$423.0M	24.9M shares	**increase of 10.0M shares**
RIG	$15.3B	6.7%	$772.9M	16.2M shares	*decrease of 2.6M shares*
STI	$11.0B	1.0%	$545.6M	30.4M shares	*decrease of 1.7M shares*
WFC	$156.0B	1.6%	$575.2M	23.8M shares	*decrease of 9.8M shares*
WY	$10.9B	3.0%	$366.3M	23.6M shares	*decrease of 6.4M shares*
XL	$6.5B	2.2%	$445.1M	23.7M shares	*decrease of 4.6M shares*

PORTFOLIO PERFORMANCE 6 MONTH

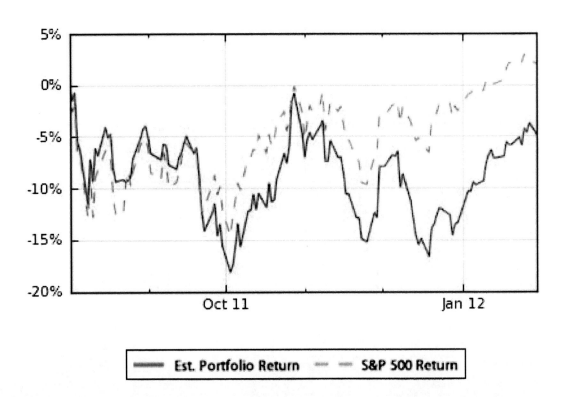

114

Renaissance Technologies

Renaissance Technologies

Renaissance Technologies is a private investment management company founded in 1982 by Jim Simons, who (correctly) believed in the potential of technical trading models.

"The advantage scientists bring into the game is less their mathematical or computational skills than their ability to think scientifically. They are less likely to accept an apparent winning strategy that might be a mere statistical fluke."

Jim Simons President Renaissance Technologies

Chances are you haven't heard of Jim Simons, which is just fine by him. Nor are you alone. Many on Wall Street, including competitors in his specialty, quantitative trading, haven't heard of Simons or of his operation, Renaissance Technologies Corp., either. And that's simply extraordinary -- because, gross or net, Simons may very well be one of the best money manager on earth. An extreme judgment? Perhaps. Certainly, there has been no end of claimants to the title. And one after another, over the past few years, these celebrated managers have either blown up or folded their tents. After big reverses, Julian Robertson closed down Tiger Management, and George Soros scaled back the activities of his Quantum Fund this year. John Meriwether's Long-Term Capital Management neatly took down the financial world in 1998. Simons, by contrast, just keeps getting better. Consider his performance over the past decade. Since its inception in March 1988, Simons' flagship $ 3.3 billion Medallion fund, has amassed annual returns of 35.6 percent, compared with 17.9 percent for the Standard & Poor's 500 index. For the 11 full years ended December 1999, Medallion's cumulative returns are an eye-popping 2,478.6 percent. Among all offshore funds over that same period, according to the database run by veteran hedge fund observer Antoine Bernheim, the next-best performer was Soros' Quantum Fund, with a 1,710.1 percent return. Simons is No. 1, says Bernheim. Ahead of George Soros. Ahead of Mark Kingdon. Ahead of Bruce Kovner. Ahead of Monroe Trout. Jim Simons is without question one of the really brilliant people working in this business, says quantitative trading star David Shaw, chairman of D.E. Shaw, which boasts returns above 50 percent this year. He is a first-rate scholar, with a genuinely scientific approach to trading. There are very few people like him. Simons surrounds himself with like minds. The headquarters of Renaissance, in the quaint town of East Setauket on New York's Long Island, resembles nothing so much as a high-powered think tank or graduate school in math and science. Operating out of a one-story wood-and-glass compound near SUNY Stony Brook, Renaissance, founded in 1982, has 140 employees, one third of whom hold Ph.D.s in hard sciences. Many have studied or taught in Stony Brook's math department, which Simons chaired from 1968 to 1976. Among their ranks: practitioners in the fields of astrophysics, number theory, computer science and computational linguistics. In notably short supply are finance types. Just two employees, including the head of trading, are Wall Street veterans. I have one guy who has a Ph.D. in finance. We don't hire people from business schools. We don't hire people from Wall Street, says Simons. We hire people who have done good science. The atmosphere is college casual, if intense - think of a perpetual exam week. Though a natty dresser, Simons sets a properly idiosyncratic tone. He has been known to show up at formal business meetings without socks, says Jerome Swartz, Simons' next-door neighbor on Long Island. Job candidates don't have to know any finance -- in fact, Wall Street experience is a black mark -- but they must present a talk on their scientific research to the entire firm before being offered a job. Most staffers seem to know little about the rest of the financial services industry, or even the hedge fund business. Asked about the performance of legendary futures trader and Renaissance rival Paul Tudor Jones, one researcher says, Who's Tudor Jones?

Company Name: Renaissance Technologies
Shares Held, Change in Shares, and Position Change as of February 1, 2012

Ticker	Mkt Cap	Div Yield	Share Value	Shares Held	Change in Shares
AAPL	$416.9B	-	$398.9M	1.0M shares	*decrease of 282.2K shares*
ALTR	$12.9B	0.8%	$170.1M	5.4M shares	**increase of 629.8K shares**
BMY	$54.7B	4.2%	$177.3M	5.6M shares	*decrease of 1.5M shares*
CL	$43.7B	2.6%	$200.4M	2.3M shares	*decrease of 360.2K shares*
CMG	$11.4B	-	$245.6M	810.7K shares	**increase of 201.9K shares**
INTC	$136.8B	3.1%	$200.8M	9.4M shares	*decrease of 3.3M shares*
JPM	$79.9B	2.7%	$167.7M	5.6M shares	**increase of 688.1K shares**
LLY	$45.3B	5.0%	$262.5M	7.1M shares	*decrease of 3.2M shares*
LO	$14.5B	4.7%	$323.6M	2.9M shares	**increase of 63.0K shares**
MCD	$100.9B	2.8%	$270.5M	3.1M shares	**increase of 620.9K shares**
MSFT	$245.0B	2.7%	$237.1M	9.5M shares	New Holding
NVO	$67.8B	1.2%	$213.6M	2.1M shares	**increase of 381.2K shares**
PCLN	$26.1B	-	$223.5M	497.2K shares	**increase of 96.5K shares**
PM	$131.3B	4.1%	$392.2M	6.3M shares	**increase of 2.7M shares**
SLB	$102.8B	1.4%	$191.1M	3.2M shares	**increase of 3.0M shares**

PORTFOLIO PERFORMANCE 6 MONTH

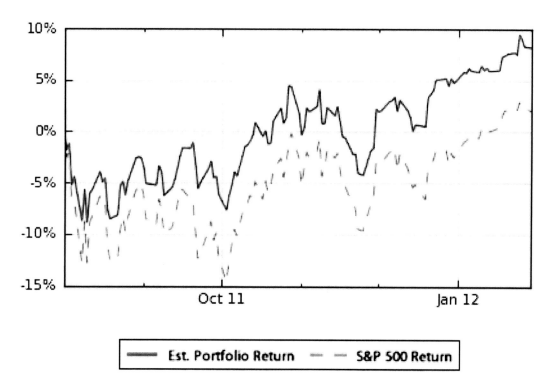

T. Boone Pickens - BP Capital Management

T. Boone Pickens - BP Capital Management

Thomas Boone Pickens, Jr. (born May 22, 1928), known as T. Boone Pickens, is an American financier who chairs the hedge fund BP Capital Management. He was a well-known takeover operator and corporate raider during the 1980s. With an estimated current net worth of about $1.4 billion, he is ranked by Forbes as the 880th-richest person in the world.

Graduated from Oklahoma State with degree in geology 1951. Started Mesa Petroleum in 1956 with $2,500. Sold to Richard Rainwater; made name with attempted takeovers of Phillips, Unocal. Now invests via energy fund BP Capital; owns water rights in Texas Panhandle. Has donated $500 million to Oklahoma State athletics, academics; $500 million to medicine.

Company Name: T. Boone Pickens - BP Capital Management
Shares Held, Change in Shares, and Position Change as of February 1, 2012

Ticker	Mkt Cap	Div Yield	Share Value	Shares Held	Change in Shares
BP	$138.0B	3.8%	$14.9M	413.4K shares	*decrease of 413.5K shares*
CHK	$14.5B	1.6%	$15.0M	585.4K shares	*decrease of 475.9K shares*
CNQ	$44.0B	0.9%	$5.7M	194.6K shares	*decrease of 103.1K shares*
DVN	$26.4B	1.1%	$8.1M	146.0K shares	New Holding
DWSN	$285.1M	-	$6.1M	257.8K shares	*decrease of 7.8K shares*
EOG	$27.9B	0.6%	$7.9M	111.0K shares	*decrease of 90.0K shares*
GST	$191.5M	-	$3.9M	1.3M shares	**increase of 61.4K shares**
HAL	$34.1B	1.0%	$3.9M	127.6K shares	*decrease of 134.4K shares*
MMR	$2.0B	-	$11.0M	1.1M shares	*decrease of 34.7K shares*
NOV	$32.8B	0.6%	$9.6M	186.7K shares	*decrease of 29.1K shares*
OXY	$81.3B	1.8%	$4.2M	58.9K shares	*decrease of 106.1K shares*
SD	$3.3B	-	$6.9M	1.2M shares	*decrease of 777.3K shares*
SU	$54.1B	1.3%	$5.6M	221.6K shares	*decrease of 124.1K shares*
WFT	$12.8B	-	$6.5M	533.5K shares	*decrease of 645.1K shares*
XOM	$411.4B	2.2%	$7.1M	97.3K shares	New Holding

PORTFOLIO PERFORMANCE 6 MONTH

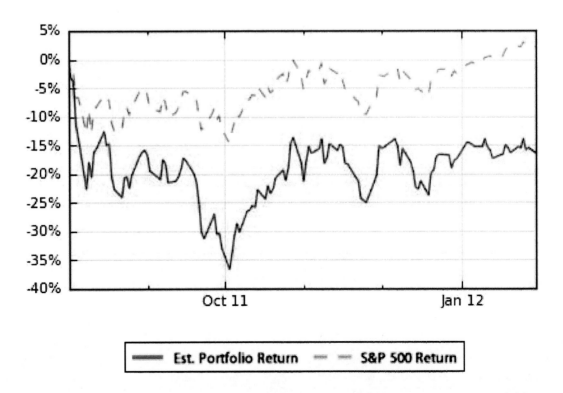

Est. Portfolio Return — — S&P 500 Return

Zacks Investment Management

Zacks Investment Management

Zacks Investment Management, a wealth management boutique, is an expert on earnings and using earnings estimates in the investment process. Zacks Investment Management, are a wholly owned subsidiary of our parent company, Zacks Investment Research, one of the largest providers of independent research in the U.S.

Zacks Investment Management, specialize in managing equity and fixed income portfolios for individual investors using a unique combination of Zacks independent research and Zacks proprietary quantitative models that have been proven year after year to deliver market-beating results.

Company Name:Zacks Investment Management
Shares Held, Change in Shares, and Position Change as of February 1, 2012

Ticker	Mkt Cap	Div Yield	Share Value	Shares Held	Change in Shares
AAPL	$416.9B	-	$15.5M	40.6K shares	*decrease of 5.2K shares*
ABX	$49.5B	1.2%	$14.0M	299.6K shares	**increase of 53.2K shares**
AGG	$	2.8%	$34.3M	311.3K shares	*decrease of 5.5K shares*
COO	$3.4B	0.1%	$12.9M	163.4K shares	*decrease of 1.9K shares*
CVX	$207.0B	3.1%	$22.8M	246.5K shares	*decrease of 4.3K shares*
DLTR	$10.0B	-	$15.1M	200.8K shares	**increase of 5.5K shares**
EMC	$52.6B	-	$13.2M	630.9K shares	**increase of 9.0K shares**
EWU	$	3.2%	$13.8M	933.6K shares	*decrease of 33.0K shares*
GOOG	$187.7B	-	$13.1M	25.4K shares	**increase of 4.3K shares**
IBM	$224.4B	1.6%	$17.4M	99.6K shares	**increase of 1.3K shares**
INTC	$136.8B	3.1%	$15.9M	745.0K shares	**increase of 14.5K shares**
KMB	$27.9B	3.9%	$14.6M	204.9K shares	**increase of 177.6K shares**
MRK	$117.5B	4.3%	$14.2M	434.3K shares	**increase of 9.3K shares**
T	$172.7B	6.0%	$16.2M	569.0K shares	**increase of 13.6K shares**
XOM	$411.4B	2.2%	$20.2M	278.2K shares	*decrease of 3.4K shares*

PORTFOLIO PERFORMANCE 6 MONTH

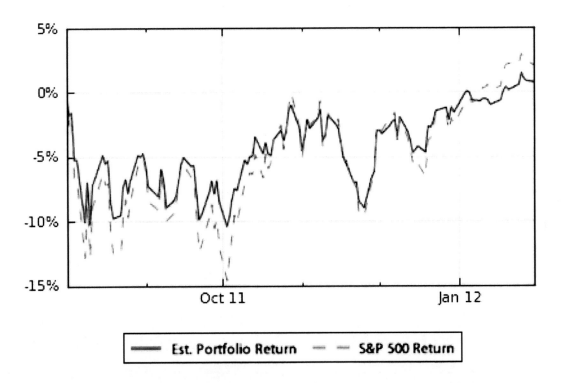

— Est. Portfolio Return   — — S&P 500 Return

Fisher Investments

Fisher Investments

Founded in 1979, Fisher Investments is a multi-billion dollar company and one of the world's largest independent investment advisory firms. Based in Woodside, CA, Fisher Investments manages assets for some of the world's wealthiest individuals, though many clients view themselves as "millionaires next door." Clients are just as likely to be retired and living off their investments as working and adding to their portfolios. Fisher Investments also serves large institutional investors, including Fortune 500 companies, foundations and endowments, and governments.

Company Name:Fisher Investments
Shares Held, Change in Shares, and Position Change as of February 1, 2012

Ticker	Mkt Cap	Div Yield	Share Value	Shares Held	Change in Shares
ABT	$85.7B	3.5%	$478.3M	9.4M shares	*decrease of 14.3K shares*
AMZN	$88.8B	-	$547.3M	2.5M shares	**increase of 7.3K shares**
BASFY	$73.6B	2.9%	$581.2M	9.5M shares	**increase of 23.7K shares**
GE	$200.9B	3.6%	$478.6M	31.4M shares	**increase of 122.1K shares**
GSK	$113.2B	4.9%	$481.4M	11.7M shares	**increase of 3.4K shares**
JNJ	$179.1B	3.5%	$685.7M	10.8M shares	**increase of 40.8K shares**
LQD	$	4.3%	$694.9M	6.2M shares	**increase of 280.8K shares**
NSRGY	$191.7B	3.0%	$525.0M	9.5M shares	*decrease of 2.3K shares*
ORCL	$143.0B	0.8%	$588.3M	20.5M shares	**increase of 22.4K shares**
RHHBY	$148.7B	2.7%	$493.6M	12.3M shares	**increase of 18.1K shares**
SI	$84.2B	3.0%	$565.1M	6.3M shares	**increase of 11.1K shares**
SLB	$102.8B	1.4%	$487.2M	8.2M shares	**increase of 25.1K shares**
SNY	$99.8B	3.6%	$483.1M	14.7M shares	*decrease of 21.5K shares*
UN	$101.3B	3.1%	$481.3M	15.3M shares	*decrease of 33.6K shares*
XOM	$411.4B	2.2%	$519.0M	7.1M shares	*decrease of 32.2K shares*

PORTFOLIO PERFORMANCE 6 MONTH

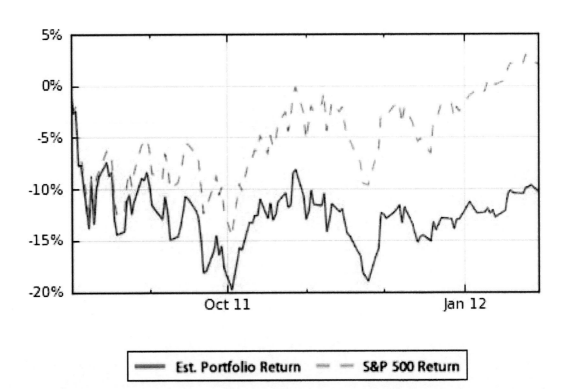

138

Tudor Investment Corporation

Tudor Investment Corporation

Tudor Investment Corporation (TIC) is a privately owned hedge fund sponsor. The firm also provides advisory services to its clients. The firm invests in the public equity and fixed income markets across the globe. It invests in the global currency and commodities markets. It employs event-driven strategies with fundamental analysis to create its equity investments. The firm makes its equity investments in the U.S., Europe, and emerging markets across the globe. Tudor Investment Corporation was founded in 1980 and is based in Greenwich, Connecticut with additional offices in Washington, District of Columbia and New York, New York.

Mr. Paul Tudor Jones II is the Chairman, Founder, Chief Executive Officer, and Controlling Principal at Tudor Investment Corporation. He founded the firm in 1980, and has operated the company continuously since 1983. Mr. Jones is a Member of the Commodity Exchange, Inc., the New York Board of Trade, Inc., the Chicago Board of Trade, and the Chicago Mercantile Exchange. In addition, he is a Director of the Cantor Fitzgerald Futures Exchange. Mr. Jones is the Founder and a Director of The Robin Hood Foundation. He is a Director of the National Fish and Wildlife Foundation and The Everglades Foundation Inc. Mr. Jones was the Chairman of the New York Cotton Exchange (which is now a division of the New York Board of Trade, Inc.) from August 1992 through June 1995. He earned a B.A. in Economics from University of Virginia.

Trading style and beliefs

As reported in Market Wizards, Jones futures trading style and beliefs are summarized as follows :

Contrarian attempt to buy and sell turning points. Keeps trying the single trade idea until he changes his mind, fundamentally. Otherwise, he keeps cutting his position size down. Then he trades the smallest amount when his trading is at its worst.

Considers himself as a premier market opportunist. When he develops an idea, he pursues it from a very-low-risk standpoint until he has been proven wrong repeatedly, or until he changes his viewpoint.

Swing trader, the best money is made at the market turns. Has missed a lot of meat in the middle, but catches a lot of tops and bottoms.

Spends his day making himself happy and relaxed. Gets out if a losing position is making him uncomfortable. Nothing's better than a fresh start. Key is to play great defense, not great offense.

Never average losers. Decreases his trading size when he is doing poorly, increase when he is trading well.

He has mental stops. If it hits that number, he is out no matter what. He uses not only price stops, but time stops.

Monitors the whole portfolio equity (risk) in realtime.

He believes prices move first and fundamentals come second.

He doesn't care about mistakes made 3 seconds ago, but what he is going to do from the next moment on.

Don't be a hero. Don't have an ego. Always question yourself and your ability. Don't ever feel that you are very good. The second you do, you are dead.

Company Name: Tudor Investment
Shares Held, Change in Shares, and Position Change as of February 1, 2012

Ticker	Mkt Cap	Div Yield	Share Value	Shares Held	Change in Shares
BAX	$31.4B	2.4%	$18.5M	329.2K shares	New Holding
CMCSA	$71.7B	1.7%	$19.0M	910.1K shares	**increase of 895.1K shares**
CTL	$23.0B	7.8%	$27.8M	838.5K shares	**increase of 683.8K shares**
EXPR	$1.9B	-	$17.4M	857.3K shares	New Holding
GCAP	$219.8M	3.2%	$14.1M	2.2M shares	No Change
GLD	$	-	$31.6M	200.0K shares	New Holding
GOOG	$187.7B	-	$17.4M	33.7K shares	*decrease of 20.4K shares*
GPRO	$3.1B	-	$12.5M	219.1K shares	**increase of 213.1K shares**
HME	$2.8B	4.2%	$11.4M	200.0K shares	New Holding
LIFE	$8.6B	-	$17.2M	447.6K shares	**increase of 442.0K shares**
PFE	$165.1B	4.1%	$20.1M	1.1M shares	New Holding
PGNX	$326.7M	-	$13.4M	2.3M shares	No Change
SBUX	$35.4B	1.4%	$11.2M	300.4K shares	New Holding
SPY	$	2.0%	$11.8M	104.0K shares	New Holding
VOD	$136.1B	5.3%	$16.0M	624.0K shares	New Holding

PORTFOLIO PERFORMANCE 6 MONTH

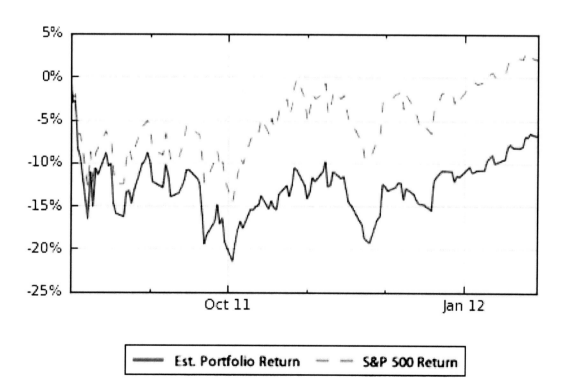

Yale University

Yale University

With a staff of twenty professionals, the Investments Office manages Yale's multi-billion Endowment, employing a broadly diversified portfolio of U.S. stocks, U.S. bonds, foreign stocks, real estate, leveraged buyouts, venture capital, and alternative investment strategies. The Yale Investments Office has widely recognized expertise in identifying and working with the world's top investors and is renowned for its creativity and innovation in the world of institutional investing, both of which have contributed to market-leading returns over the past twenty years.

Company Name: Yale University
Shares Held, Change in Shares, and Position Change as of February 1, 2012

Ticker	Mkt Cap	Div Yield	Share Value	Shares Held	Change in Shares
AREX	$966.3M	-	$1.6M	95.6K shares	No Change
EEM	$	1.9%	$84.4M	2.4M shares	**increase of 879.0K shares**
EFA	$	3.3%	$39.0M	816.6K shares	**increase of 650.6K shares**
ONE	$956.8M	-	$1.6M	97.1K shares	No Change
SPY	$	2.0%	$49.2M	434.6K shares	**increase of 413.6K shares**
TIVO	$1.2B	-	$798.1K	85.5K shares	New Holding
VWO	$	2.2%	$80.9M	2.3M shares	New Holding
WWW	$1.8B	1.2%	$685.4K	20.6K shares	No Change

PORTFOLIO PERFORMANCE 6 MONTH

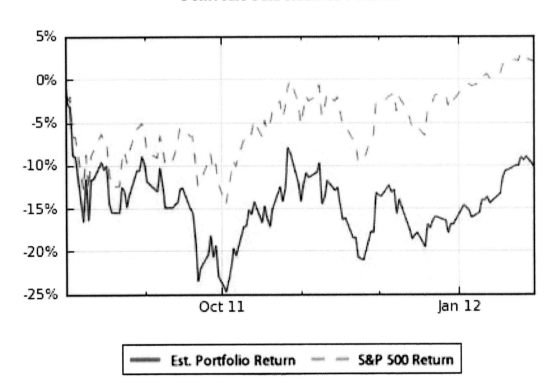

Pabrai Funds

Pabrai Funds

Mohnish Pabrai is an Indian-American businessman, investor and philanthropist.

In June 2007 he made headlines by bidding US$650,100 on eBay for a charity lunch with Warren Buffett.

Pabrai has high regards for Warren Buffett and admits that his investment style is copied from Buffett and others. He has written a book on his investing style: "The Dhandho Investor: The Low - Risk Value Method to High Returns".

Another book by Pabrai is "Mosaic: Perspectives on Investing". In this book Pabrai has distilled the Warren Buffett method of investing down to a few points.

Company Name: Pabrai Funds
Shares Held, Change in Shares, and Position Change as of February 1, 2012

Ticker	Mkt Cap	Div Yield	Share Value	Shares Held	Change in Shares
ATSG	$381.8M	-	$581.7K	134.3K shares	*decrease of 1.1M shares*
BAC	$73.8B	0.6%	$43.2M	7.1M shares	New Holding
BIP	$3.8B	4.8%	$43.0M	1.8M shares	*decrease of 1.8K shares*
BPO	$8.7B	3.2%	$32.5M	2.4M shares	*decrease of 51 shares*
BRK.B	$186.5B	-	$673.0K	9.5K shares	*decrease of 400 shares*
BRP	$892.0M	-	$1.6M	241.6K shares	No Change
CRESY	$647.0M	4.8%	$11.1M	1.0M shares	*decrease of 258.5K shares*
CSE	$1.9B	0.6%	$17.3M	2.8M shares	No Change
HNR	$234.1M	-	$475.6K	55.5K shares	*decrease of 15.9K shares*
PKX	$32.7B	2.0%	$326.9K	4.3K shares	*decrease of 66.4K shares*
PNCL	$15.3M	-	$5.8M	2.0M shares	No Change
POT	$40.7B	1.2%	$34.4M	796.0K shares	*decrease of 198.9K shares*
WFC	$156.0B	1.6%	$29.5M	1.2M shares	**increase of 850.7K shares**
ZINC	$493.7M	-	$10.1M	1.4M shares	No Change

PORTFOLIO PERFORMANCE 6 MONTH

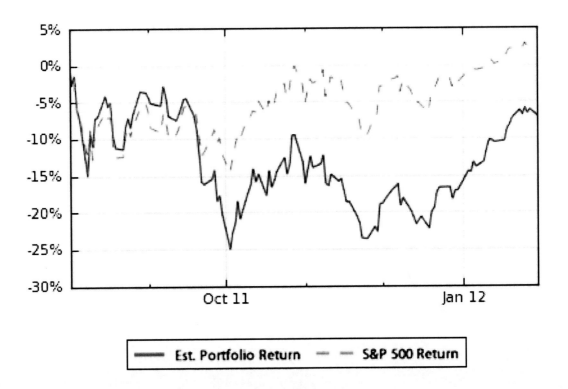

Baupost Group

Baupost Group

Seth Klarman is the founder and president of the Baupost Group, a Boston-based private investment partnership, and the author of a book on value investing.

Before founding Baupost, Klarman worked for Max Heine and Michael Price of the Mutual Shares fund (now a part of Franklin Templeton Investments). He founded the Baupost Group in 1982, which managed USD 22 Billion as of 2010. Despite his unconventional strategies, he has consistently achieved high returns. He is a very conservative investor, and often holds a significant amounts of cash in his investment portfolios, sometimes in excess of 50% of the total. He often makes unusual investments, buying unpopular assets while they are undervalued, using complex derivatives, and buying put options. Klarman typically keeps a low profile, rarely speaking in public or granting interviews.

Company Name: Baupost Group
Shares Held, Change in Shares, and Position Change as of February 1, 2012

Ticker	Mkt Cap	Div Yield	Share Value	Shares Held	Change in Shares
ALR	$1.8B	-	$60.9M	3.1M shares	No Change
ANV	$3.3B	-	$125.3M	3.5M shares	**increase of 121.7K shares**
AVEO	$572.2M	-	$77.0M	5.0M shares	**increase of 567.0K shares**
BBEP	$1.1B	9.0%	$43.5M	2.5M shares	No Change
BP	$138.0B	3.8%	$495.6M	13.7M shares	**increase of 8.2M shares**
ELOS	$376.5M	-	$39.6M	4.0M shares	**increase of 163.9K shares**
ENZN	$342.7M	-	$63.4M	9.0M shares	No Change
GNW	$3.8B	-	$57.4M	10.0M shares	New Holding
HPQ	$55.5B	1.7%	$465.8M	20.8M shares	New Holding
MSFT	$245.0B	2.7%	$298.7M	12.0M shares	No Change
NWS	$49.8B	1.0%	$66.8M	4.3M shares	New Holding
NWSA	$	1.0%	$325.7M	21.0M shares	**increase of 2.0M shares**
PDLI	$893.9M	9.4%	$86.8M	15.6M shares	**increase of 6.4M shares**
THRX	$1.6B	-	$286.5M	14.2M shares	**increase of 1.3M shares**
VSAT	$1.9B	-	$349.8M	10.5M shares	**increase of 448.5K shares**

PORTFOLIO PERFORMANCE 6 MONTH

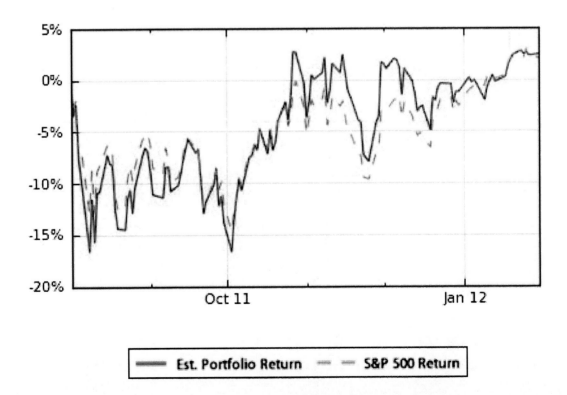

Est. Portfolio Return — — S&P 500 Return

Harvard Management Company

Harvard Management Company

Harvard Management Company (HMC) seeks to provide world-class investment management focused solely on generating strong results to support the educational and research objectives of Harvard University. HMC's history of solid endowment returns has opened Harvard's doors to students who otherwise would not have been able to attend and has helped finance significant discoveries in scientific research. HMC investment strategy combines long-term goals with dynamic management. Today, HMC is using innovative new strategies to expand the boundaries of HMC portfolio for the future.

Company Name: Harvard Management
Shares Held, Change in Shares, and Position Change as of February 1, 2012

Ticker	Mkt Cap	Div Yield	Share Value	Shares Held	Change in Shares
AMX	$80.7B	1.2%	$21.7M	984.7K shares	increase of 32.8K shares
ECH	$	1.7%	$25.0M	470.0K shares	increase of 104.8K shares
EWW	$	1.3%	$23.6M	482.6K shares	increase of 304.6K shares
EWY	$	1.2%	$42.0M	901.0K shares	increase of 120.7K shares
EWZ	$	2.3%	$256.6M	4.9M shares	increase of 521.8K shares
FXI	$	2.0%	$68.4M	2.2M shares	increase of 1.4M shares
GR	$15.5B	0.9%	$67.0M	555.0K shares	New Holding
GSG	$	-	$11.5M	380.0K shares	No Change
IDX	$	1.5%	$38.1M	1.5M shares	increase of 619.9K shares
INP	$	-	$44.9M	835.0K shares	increase of 515.5K shares
IVV	$	2.0%	$10.3M	90.9K shares	*decrease of 19.5K shares*
PEB	$1.1B	2.2%	$40.6M	2.6M shares	No Change
RSX	$	1.9%	$33.2M	1.3M shares	increase of 13.5K shares
SCJ	$	2.4%	$12.6M	237.5K shares	increase of 27.5K shares
TUR	$	2.4%	$10.8M	227.7K shares	increase of 179.9K shares

PORTFOLIO PERFORMANCE 6 MONTH

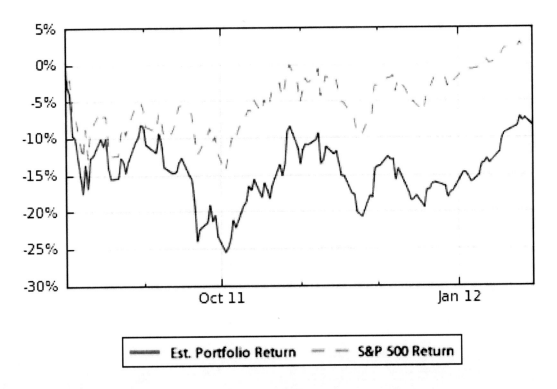

168

RECOMMENDED READING

Recommended Reading

How I made $2,000,000 in the Stock Market
By: Nicolas Darvas

Wall Street: The Other Las Vegas
By: Nicolas Darvas

You Can Still Make it in the Market
By: Nicolas Darvas

How I Made Money Using the Nicolas Darvas System,
Which Made Him $2,000,000 in the Stock Market
By Steve Burns

The Battle for Investment Survival
by Gerald M. Loeb

The Psychology Of The Stock Market
by G. C. Selden

The Science of Getting Rich
by Wallace D. Wattles

Think and Grow Rich
by Napoleon Hill

TRADING SMART: 92 Tools, Methods, Helpful Hints and High Probability Trading
Strategies to Help You Succeed at Forex, Futures, Commodities and Stock Market Trading
By Jim Wyckoff

Rules Used by Profitable Traders for Investing in Gold and Silver
By Arik Zahb

Available at www.bnpublishing.net

CPSIA information can be obtained at www.ICGtesting.com
Printed in the USA
LVOW112008011112

305446LV00014B/84/P

9 781607 964124